DYLAN & ME

50 YEARS OF ADVENTURES

DYLAN & ME

50 YEARS OF ADVENTURES

LOUIE KEMP

with Kinky Friedman

WESTROSE PRESS
Los Angeles, CA

WestRose Press
Los Angeles, CA
www.dylanandme.com
louie@dylanandme.com

Dylan & Me: 50 Years of Adventures is a trademark of the author and is used by the publisher with permission.

All photos, including those with credits, constitute an extension of this copyright page.

Lyrics to the song "Some Get the Chair," by Larry Kegan and Gene LaFond, which appear on page 22, are reprinted with permission of Gene LaFond.

Printed in the United States of America and Canada.

ISBN: 978-1-733012-1-2 (hardcover)
            978-1-7330012-0-5 (paperback)
            978-1-7330012-2-9 (e-book)
            978-1-7330012-3-6 (signed hardcover & bookmark)

First Edition

10 9 8 7 6 5 4 3 2 1

Cover and interior design:
Redwood Publishing & Albertine Book Design

DEDICATION

To my parents,
Abe and Frieda Kemp,
of blessed memory,

To all my ancestors
upon whose shoulders I stand,
who have made it possible
for me to be here,

To my seed and my seed's seed
in all the generations to come.

DYLAN & ME

50 YEARS OF ADVENTURES

CONTENTS

ACKNOWLEDGMENTS

SPECIAL THANKS TO. . .

. . . Larry Kegan, of blessed memory

. . . Cantor Braverman, of blessed memory, who prepared me for my Bar Mitzvah and for life

. . . Tzvi Small, of blessed memory, who insisted that I write this book

. . . Gary Shafner

. . . my sister, Sharon Kemp

. . . my daughter, Rachel, and her husband, Daniel, who recently got married (Mazel tov!)

. . . Harold Shapiro, of blessed memory

. . . Nachman Noam, "I keep my deals."

. . . Rabbi and Rebetzin Zushe and Zissi Cunin of Chabad of Pacific Palisades, who took the seeds I planted and grew them into an orchid

. . . Rabbi Noah Wineberg, of blessed memory, founder of Aish HaTorah, who allowed me to be his founding partner in Aish's Discovery Program

. . . Kinky, for his help and for being Kinky

. . . Zohar Kantor—writer, editor, sea captain

. . . Laura Ross, my great editor and book mentor

. . . Sara Stratton, my VERY special publishing concierge

. . . Larry David, for having been a good next-door neighbor with whom I exchanged keys, and who told me, "You can't move! You are the best neighbor I have ever had—even better than Kramer!"

. . . Herzl Camp, where Bobby and I spent five glorious summers and where our adventures started

. . . and, of course, Bobby. And G-D.

FOREWORD

Why is this book different from all other Bob Dylan books?

The answer is quite simple. It is because these stories are told by the only other guy who was there. His name is Louie Kemp and he and Bobby Zimmerman met at summer camp when he was eleven years old. For the next fifty years, the two amigos maintained a heroic friendship. That's a lot longer than most marriages last, or relationships, cars, refrigerators, fish, claims to fame, or anything else I can think of.

The two friends proceeded to travel the world, gaining renown in their respective fields and becoming—beyond doubt—the two most successful dropouts in the history of the University of Minnesota. Yet, they continually came back together to share epic adventures, most of which have never been written about until now, and certainly not from this close up.

When I first heard some of Louie's stories, I thought, *This is what happens when your best friend from childhood becomes a superstar.* As I heard more of his tales, I began to feel the tug of something much bigger and just as credible.

In *Dylan & Me,* Louie has faithfully and unselfconsciously written nothing less than a historical work, a modern-day version of Tom Sawyer's adventures with Huckleberry Finn. Bobby Zimmerman from Hibbing, Minnesota, is Tom, of course—the ringleader and dreamer. Louie Kemp from Duluth, Minnesota, though he sees himself as his friend's protector, is the more naïve and innocent of the two. Their uniquely American escapades, both before and after Bobby became "Bob," make for fun, entertaining, and very enlightening reading—especially the way Louie tells them.

Congratulations on wrestling this big, uniquely American story to the ground and squeezing it between the covers of a book. Or, as Bob might say (and often did), "Good work, Louie."

—Kinky Friedman
Echo Hill Ranch, Texas

ONE
___

Bobby on the Roof

It was at summer camp in northern Wisconsin in 1953 that I first met Bobby Zimmerman from Hibbing. He was twelve years old and he had a guitar. He would go around telling everybody that he was going to be a rock-and-roll star. I was eleven and I believed him.

Even at that tender age, I could see that most of the other kids weren't really buying it. None of them would say so to his face, but I could hear them making comments and laughing behind his back, and it bugged me. Why didn't they see what I saw? Maybe I was the most gullible kid at Herzl Camp, or maybe it was the beginning of a beautiful friendship. Maybe a little bit of both.

Ultimately, of course, it didn't matter whether the other kids bought into Bobby's dream, or whether I did. The only thing that mattered was that Bobby believed in it. And that's why it came true.

Don't get me wrong. Bobby was very popular with the other kids, especially the girls. This was due in part to his natural charm, but also to his talent. He was not just the kid with the guitar; he could *play* the thing. He was a maverick and a freethinker, always fun to be with, challenging, and sometimes very disruptive.

1

When the counselors came up with a good idea for an activity, Bobby came up with a better one. He was a prankster who liked to stir things up. Add to that a hip, edgy sense of humor and a surprisingly well-honed ability to be provocative, and that was Bobby. He always knew when a dose of sarcasm was called for, or when a little bit of ruckus was needed—and I was down with all of it. Bobby was my kind of guy!

Bobby and I teamed up with a third kid in our cabin, Larry Kegan, who, like Bobby, was talented and deeply into music. He was also a natural-born hell-raiser. Larry was fun and passionate, but, as the boxing champ at Herzl, I was the protector of our little band.

I'd been well prepared for the role by my father, Abe, an old Golden Glover who handed me my first pair of gloves in our backyard when I was nine, and said, "Put these on. I'm going to teach you to box."

When I'd done as I was told, he said, "OK, now put your hands up. Ready?"

"Yes …" I said, and then—BOOM—he hit me in the kisser so hard he knocked me down.

"Why'd you do that?" I whined, looking up at him.

"So nobody else ever will," he said.

Our lessons continued from there, covering the techniques, skills, and style of boxing. He taught me how to coordinate my feet and hands, dance around my opponent, and use a straight left jab to set up a powerful right. I picked it all up naturally and it turned out I was pretty strong and pretty fast on my feet. If Muhammad Ali could float like a butterfly and sting like a bee, Louie Kemp could dance like Michael Jackson and hit like a frozen mackerel.

After about a year of training, Dad told me I was ready to protect myself.

"I don't ever want to see you start a fight," he told me, "but if anybody starts up with you, show them what you can do. And I want you to carry on the family tradition of sticking up for the little guy against any bully who comes along."

"OK, Dad," I said. And that's exactly what I've done ever since.

Maybe you're getting an inkling of why the three of us were every counselor's worst nightmare—not quite juvenile delinquents, but close enough … and proud of it.

One night, Bobby, Larry, and I were feeling kind of restless; we couldn't sleep. So we started hatching a plan for dealing with our archenemies, the kids in the next cabin. In our not-so-humble opinion, these kids were just too perfect. They never broke the rules, never got into any kind of trouble. Something had to be done about them.

After hours of plotting, scheming, and bullshitting, we decided on a clandestine nighttime attack on the enemy cabin. It's easy to see now that this wasn't a very sophisticated or well-thought-out effort, but it seemed like a great idea at the time.

In the dead of night, we made our move. Armed with nothing but three pilfered cans of the counselor's shaving cream, we sneaked into the enemy cabin, where the forces of good all appeared to be sleeping. We crept stealthily from bunk to bunk, discharging dollops of shaving cream upon the heads of the entire horde. The only hard part for me was trying not to burst into peals of laughter every time I stole a glance at Bobby. He was very meticulous about his shaving-cream placement, and quite artistic in his designs—the natural-born Van Gogh of Barbasol. The objects of our efforts slept through the whole thing.

Having completed our mission, we split as fast as hell back to our cabin, jumped into our bunks, and composed ourselves as best we could into the image of three innocent kids lost in dreamland.

Of course it wasn't long before our whole bunk was jolted awake by the sound of shouting and the flicker of flashlights outside our screened windows. Sure enough, dark figures were headed in our direction. We three knuckleheads went back to feigning sleep, praying that the Angel of Death would pass over our cabin.

This, alas, was not to be. The shaving cream had barely dried on the foreheads of our whiny little foes when the counselors made a beeline for the likely culprits: us.

As our bunkmates looked on silently, our captors marched us out of the cabin and along a dirt road that led into the woods. When I finally got up the nerve to steal a glance at Bobby, I could see that his signature smirk was intact. That cheered me up a little in spite of the cold and the silver-dollar-sized mosquitos that kept dive-bombing us.

When we'd gone on for what seemed like miles (but

was probably just a few hundred yards), the counselors told us to sit down on some logs, and they started building a bonfire. Were they were planning to burn us at the stake? As they were busy gathering up kindling, the three of us looked at each other; we weren't taking any chances. Without exchanging a word, we took off into the darkness like three little Jewish bats out of hell.

It wasn't long before we came upon one of the counselors' cars parked by the side of the road. The Lord was with us; the keys were in the ignition. Without giving it a second thought, I slid behind the wheel, Bobby jumped into shotgun position, and Larry—always the jock—vaulted into the backseat just as I gunned her out of there in a cloud of dust. I had to be the best eleven-year-old wheelman in the state.

"Stop ... STOP! You little monsters, get back here!" was all we could hear as the counselors—probably not more than teens themselves—got smaller and smaller in the rearview mirror. Bobby was laughing, which made me laugh, which in turn made Larry laugh. Larry had a beautiful laugh; it almost sounded like he was singing.

Herzl Camp disappeared in an instant and we found ourselves on a dark stretch of deserted highway. The laughter sputtered out and Larry and I exchanged worried glances in the rearview mirror as I slowed the car to thirty and tried to think. Was it possible that our little shaving-cream raid had somehow transformed itself into Grand Theft Auto? I stole a glimpse at Bobby, and found him looking straight ahead with a determined expression on his face that seemed to say, *Let's keep driving forever.*

Eventually, of course, we turned back to face the music, and found ourselves in front of a very angry rabbi who threatened to send us home the next day. Luckily for us, he was one of those rare, generous souls who believe in second chances ... sometimes even third chances. In retrospect, I am very glad he didn't make good on his threat, as it would have deprived me of some of my fondest memories of childhood.

Many years later, when the subject came up, Bob summed up that riotous summer with a rhetorical question: "Can you imagine," he mused, "if there had been four hundred campers like the three of us?"

The following summer, back at Herzl with my pals, I witnessed an event that could vie for a legit place in American musical history: the 1954 version of the camp's Talent Night. It was, to the best of my knowledge, the first public performance by the prototypical Bob Dylan.

Quite often over that summer, I joined small groups of kids in the activities room as they'd gather around Bobby to listen to him play his guitar or pound the keys of the old piano and sing Jerry Lee Lewis-style. Some days, he'd play Little Richard. But Talent Night was special. It was the night when the entire camp—more than four hundred kids, plus rabbis, counselors, and staff—would assemble to witness the best skits, magic acts, and musical numbers we could muster. It would be Bobby's largest and most attentive audience to date. Perhaps it would provide a hint of what the future held.

Bobby and Larry had decided to perform together, with Bobby on piano. As they looked out at a sea of camp whites, their all-black outfits provided a sharp, rather sinister contrast. There was also some question about the appropriateness of the song they'd selected. Was it really suitable to sing a hard-driving blues number for kids as young as eight or nine? I, of course, loved it.

The tune was called "Annie Had a Baby," and started out, "Annie had a baby, can't work no more ..." and went on to list the various things Annie had to do instead of work, such as "walk with the baby, talk to the baby, sleep with the baby," etc.

It wasn't exactly "Kumbaya." When confronted about his choice of material, Bobby responded tersely and typically: "They're squares," he said. In any case, the boy who would be Dylan had made his debut, and—trust me on this—he'd nailed it.

Another performance I remember fondly took place on a warm afternoon a few summers later, in 1957. This was the traditional day when the campers took on the roles of the counselors. The idea was to teach us responsibility, leadership, and cooperation—all qualities that my two friends and I generally lacked. Bobby took the place of Shlomo, the music director. Though he'd often beaten the poor old piano to death with impromptu performances inside the activities room, Bobby had never played his guitar on top of the building. Now, seven years before *Fiddler on the Roof* would open on Broadway, he proceeded to do just that.

All day long, silhouetted against the sun, Bobby played every rock and blues song anybody had ever heard of, and lots that we hadn't. Larry and I kept him supplied with water and requests as, all day long, kids would stop by to listen in the courtyard below. Seeing Bobby on the roof in full performance mode, like a maestro at Carnegie Hall, convinced me that nothing could, would, or should ever stop him. He was our fiddler on the roof and this would become the indelible image of the last days of our childhood.

Bobby didn't look anything like the vapidly handsome blond pop stars of the day; he looked like a skinny little Jewish kid who'd never be anybody's bet to conquer the world. But that's exactly what he would do.

TWO

"Oh Boy"

Although he had moved with his family to Hibbing when he was six, Bobby often spent weekends in our hometown of Duluth, Minnesota. Duluth is a unique city built into the hills overlooking Lake Superior, the largest freshwater lake in the world. It has a thriving Jewish community and Bobby spent his early years in the heart of it, on Third Avenue East between Fifth and Sixth Streets, just blocks away from two synagogues that everybody called the Third Street Shul and the Fourth Street Synagogue.

Bobby's forebears had been founding members of the first one, an Orthodox synagogue formally known as Adas Israel Congregation. During a visit to Duluth in the 1980s, Bob and I went for evening prayers there and spent the latter part of the evening chatting with a group of elderly men who had known his parents and grandparents well. He enjoyed listening to their stories, and seemed to take personal pride in the contributions his family had made to the community. He may have grown up in Hibbing, but Bob's roots in Duluth are deep and strong.

Mark Twain famously said, "The coldest winter I ever spent was a summer in Duluth." But for us North Country boys, the outdoors beckoned whatever the season. There was always a lot to do in Duluth for two kids with an endless supply of energy to burn. Summer days were spent throwing around the football in the big park across the street from my house or going fishing with some of the neighborhood kids. Sometimes a buddy of ours from Herzl Camp, Steve Friedman, would join us. When the minor league baseball team, the Duluth Dukes, was playing at Wade Stadium, we'd hitch a ride to West Duluth to see the game. Perennially short of the cost of a ticket, we'd join up with the "Knothole Gang" behind the wooden fence at center field. After knocking out a few knots in the wood, we'd take turns peering through, then give up our spot and go to the back of the line. If something significant happened, we'd hear the crowd going wild but had to rely on the guys at the fence to provide the play-by-play for the rest of us Knotholers.

In the winter, we spent countless hours building snow forts, hurling snowballs at one another, and sledding down the big hill in the park on our toboggans. One day, a bunch of us were standing out on my front lawn and Bobby began reciting an original poem off the top of his head. It was a teasing bit of doggerel about one of the neighborhood kids—not at all mean-spirited—and it had us all howling with laughter. Bobby could make friends with anyone, charm anyone, while always being just exactly himself.

When we were about eight years old, Butchy and Corky, two of the kids we ran with, came over with a cigarette they had lifted from their mother's purse. We were huddled in the garage, trying to figure out how to light the thing, when my sister Sharon passed by and saw us. Being a typical big sister, she immediately ran off to tattle, and the next thing I knew, my mother came strolling into the garage, her purse dangling from her arm. She was wearing a smile so big it terrified us.

"Oh, you guys want to smoke?" she asked cheerfully. "Great! Let's have a smoking party!"

As we stood there gaping at her, she dug into her purse and pulled out a cigarette for each of us and then quickly struck a match and ignited them in turn. As we awkwardly attempted to draw in the smoke, she offered guidance.

"No, no," she said, "that's not how big people smoke. You have to *inhale*. You have to swallow the smoke."

Within seconds, Butchy, Corky, and I were doubled over in coughing fits while my mother continued to encourage us to puff away and inhale as deeply as we could. Soon, three little tough guys were splayed out on the floor of the garage, gasping for air, tears running down our cheeks. The smoke in the garage had grown so thick we could barely see my mother, who was still grinning madly.

"This is so much fun," she said. "We really should have smoking parties more often!"

Needless to say, the first time I ever smoked a cigarette was also the last.

Maybe this was related and maybe not, but one day, I came home from school, dropped my books on the kitchen table, and was about to go to the park to play when my mother ambushed me.

Again, she had a suspiciously wide grin on her face as she said, "Congratulations!"

I figured I must be in trouble for something, but I couldn't for the life of me think what it might be.

"For ... what?" I asked with trepidation.

"You have a job!" she said triumphantly. "You are the new janitor at the Duluth Playhouse."

"I am?"

It turned out my mother had packed up ten pounds of smoked Lake Superior trout and carried it over to the director of the place. After thanking him for the great work he was doing on behalf of Duluth's artistic community, she'd said, "By the way, I have a wonderfully resourceful eleven-year-old son who would benefit greatly from being around fine, artistic people. Would you be so kind as to offer him a position cleaning up and helping out around your beautiful playhouse?"

The man was clearly impressed by my mother's interest in her child's development—or maybe it was the trout, which always seemed to cast a spell of its own—but he said yes.

I was paid twenty-five cents an hour, and when I got my first paycheck, Mom took me downtown to the First National Bank and helped me open my first savings account.

That wasn't the last time my mother served as my employment agent. A couple years later, she congratulated me again, for having landed yet another job without realizing it: I was to be a page at the Duluth Library, at a salary of thirty-five cents an hour. You might call these jobs "menial," but let me tell you, they formed the work ethic I'd carry with me for the rest of my life. My parents understood that being around productive people and having a job to do would serve me well. As usual, they were dead right.

In spite of our shenanigans, I like to think that on the whole, my pals and I were pretty good kids. We did tend to go a little overboard around the Fourth of July, when Bobby would come to town and we would terrorize the neighborhood by lighting cherry bombs and shooting our BB guns. But on most days, we didn't do too much damage to ourselves or anybody else.

I did have a reputation as a tough guy around school, though, after I won a few schoolyard fights thanks to my father's training. Duluth Central High was a pretty tough place, full of kids from various backgrounds—including a couple straight out of Red Wing, the state's juvenile reform school—so it was good to have a reputation as somebody not to mess with.

One day, after my last class, I was at my locker when I heard some sort of commotion. I looked down the crowded hallway and saw a kid streaking toward me like he was on fire, followed by one of the bigger guys in our class, who was screaming, "I'm going to kill you, you little punk!" The smaller kid happened to be a friend of mine by the name of Stan, who'd transferred over from East High, a much tamer school. Luckily, he reached me before getting tackled, and I shoved him behind me and stood up as tall as I could.

"What's your problem?" I said to the tough guy when he skidded to a stop in front of me.

"That little creep was hustling my girlfriend," he grunted. "He's gonna die."

Keeping my voice calm, and keeping a hand on Stan, I explained that the "little creep" was my friend Stan, that he was new to Central, and that he'd probably had no idea whose girl he was chatting with.

"Get outta the way, Louie," the big guy said. "I don't want any trouble with you."

"Well, I can't let you kill my friend," I reasoned. "If you want him, you'll have to go through me."

As brave as this guy was when it came to chasing after little guys, it turned out, he didn't want to tangle with me. He shot one more killer look at Stan, then shook my hand, turned on his heel, and walked away muttering to himself.

Stan is a good guy who grew up to be one of the most successful dentists in Los Angeles, and I've been protecting underdogs ever since.

My parents liked Bobby, and he had an open invitation to stay at our house whenever he was in Duluth. He was never anything but respectful when he did so.

Like any other James Dean-inspired teenager living in a small town, Bobby grew more restless the older he got.

When he couldn't take it anymore, he'd bum a ride or hop a Greyhound from Hibbing to Duluth in search of a little action. The minute he arrived, we'd take my dad's car and head out to the East End to grab burgers at the London Inn Drive-in, the primo hangout for the youth of Duluth. It didn't matter what clique you belonged to, everyone in that parking lot was free to have a good time, flirt, and gather intel about who might be having a house party and when. Most of the parties we went to were thrown by friends of mine from within the Jewish community.

In 1958, when Bobby was almost seventeen, we were introduced to a different aspect of the social scene: an annual youth-group event called the "Beau Dance," to which the girls invited the boys. The two girls who invited us were cousins; my date was Pam and Bobby's was Kay.

The semiformal affair was held at the Saint Paul Hotel, and I recall that we had each gotten our dates wrist corsages. Every guy in the place (including me) was wearing a suit and tie—except for Bobby. He wore black pants, a black jacket, and an open-collared pink shirt with ruffles down the center. And sunglasses.

I'm still friends with Pam, but I don't know what became of Bobby's date, Kay. What I remember about her is that she came up to me toward the end of the dance and said, "Your friend Bobby doesn't talk much, does he?"

"When he has something to say, he speaks," I replied.

As we grew more interested in expanding our knowledge of "social studies"—i.e., girls—we ventured farther and farther afield. We often ended up in Saint Paul, where

our partner in crime, Larry Kegan, lived. By this time, the
three of us looked (and sometimes behaved) like a younger
version of the Wild Bunch. Gamely, we took trains some
150 miles south in order to fray welcome mats across the
Twin Cities, where a lot of the Herzl Camp kids lived. If
none of them were throwing a party, they'd let us tag along
to one thrown by somebody they knew. To us, Saint Paul
and Minneapolis were alternate names for paradise.

Sometimes Bobby would stay with his cousins in the
Highland Park area of Saint Paul, but usually, we would
all crash at a friend's house together. Eventually, one of our
camp friends informed us that we were no longer welcome
at his place.

"You can't run around with those wild boys anymore,"
his mother had declared. "Kemp, Kegan, and Zimmerman.
They'll get you into trouble."

Many years later, that guy told me his mom had amend-
ed her opinion.

"I guess the wild boys did the best," she said. "I should
have let you hang around with them."

Open houses were all the rage back then. If word got
out that you were giving a party, you never knew who might
show up. Even so, they tended to be heavily chaperoned.
There was no real dress code, but almost everybody dressed
nicely. We were the only ones in black leather jackets and
jeans. These were sedate, suburban affairs that hardly lived
up to the term *party*—that is, until Bobby showed up.

He'd walk in and not look at anybody, just head straight
for the piano. There was almost always a piano.

If the presiding adults had the notion that he might play show tunes or classical pieces or parlor sing-alongs, they were soon disabused of that notion. When Bobby began playing, a kind of sea change occurred in the room. People gravitated toward this sudden, new source of energy as Bobby pounded out pulsing, graphic rock-and-roll songs that made "Annie Had a Baby" from Herzl's Talent Night seem like a nursery rhyme by contrast. While he never played his own songs, he owned every song he covered.

After a few bruising numbers, Bobby would slip seamlessly into Jerry Lee Lewis mode. Girls with stars in their eyes visibly swooned, while the chaperones huddled in corners, discussing the deteriorating situation in worried tones. It was usually when Bobby started screaming out lyrics and pounding the piano with the heels of his boots that they stepped in and gave him the hook, and—sadly—he, Larry, and I were hustled unceremoniously out of yet another house. At that point, it was the chaperones doing most of the shouting.

This pattern repeated itself all over Duluth, Saint Paul, and Minneapolis, but we couldn't have cared less. More often than not, some hip girls who'd dug our scene would follow us out and we'd all end up laughing like it was the biggest joke in the world.

Sometimes, I'd take a stab at trying to smooth things over with the adults.

"This is the music of our generation," I would say. "It's called rock-and-roll, and it's being played all over the country. Why not give it a chance? You might even like it."

Bobby wasn't nearly so diplomatic. He'd save his best verbal shots for just the moment when I was starting to make headway by being courteous and reasonable.

"We've been kicked out of better places than this," he'd declare. "Just wait till I'm a big star; we'll get the last laugh."

And believe it or not, I think we actually did.

The most important show to Bobby that year, though, was not one of his own performances; it was a show he seemed to know he would never get to see again. The date was January 31, 1959. It was a Saturday night and—with the windchill—the temperature in Duluth was minus forty-four degrees. The car we drove was my dad's '58 metallic-blue Buick. Bobby was seventeen, I was sixteen, and we were on our way to see what would be one of Buddy Holly's last concerts. He was twenty-two and it was just three days before he, Ritchie Valens, and the Big Bopper would perish in a plane crash while taking off in an Iowa blizzard. (Another great, Waylon Jennings, would have been on that list, had he not given up his seat to the Big Bopper.)

To this day, whenever Buddy Holly's classic "Oh Boy" comes on the radio, I feel the hairs on the back of my neck snap to attention. The words seem to be emanating from his soul straight to my heart. This was my favorite song all through high school.

Bobby's musical interest was much wider and deeper than mine. Even as a child, he faithfully listened to late-night radio stations from the South, something that Buddy Holly had been doing in Lubbock, Texas, just a few years before. When I think about it, there never seemed to be a time when Bobby had not been a big fan of Buddy's. There is no doubt that the rock-and-roll pioneer was a seminal influence in his musical life.

There were many similarities between Buddy and Bobby, but one that Bobby probably wasn't aware of was that they each had a high school girlfriend named Echo. It's widely known that one of Bob's classic songs, "Girl from the North Country," was about his girlfriend, Echo Helstrom.

We arrived at the Duluth National Guard Armory for something called the Winter Dance Party, and found the tickets to be pretty pricey, ranging from a buck twenty-five all the way up to two dollars. We pooled our resources and shoved our way in, working our way through the dancing, partying throng of two thousand excited, writhing young people. With Bobby in the lead, we snaked our way right up to the edge of the stage, mere feet away from Buddy as he performed.

As still as a statue, Bobby stood there mesmerized, never taking his eyes off of Buddy. Perhaps time has embellished my memory of that night, but Buddy seemed to be smiling down on Bobby with an almost celestial countenance. At one point, he nodded to Bobby, seemingly as if he knew his own remaining time was brief and that Bobby would one day take up his mantle as one of the greatest musical artists in the world. Only four years later, Bobby would write "Blowin' in the Wind," and start fulfilling that prophecy.

I have always believed that a spiritual connection of some kind was forged that night between Buddy Holly and Bobby Zimmerman, though no one in the crowd was aware of it. I only know what I saw, and it looked a lot like a torch being passed.

THREE

Larry Gets the Chair

It was Herzl Camp that brought Bobby, Larry, and me together, but it was music that sealed the bond of our little brotherhood—particularly between Bobby and Larry.

On Christmas Eve in 1956, when most kids were waiting for Santa Claus to come down the chimney, Bobby, Larry, and their pal Howie Rutman walked into the Terlinde Music Shop in Saint Paul, Minnesota. They gave the man behind the counter five bucks to record a 78-rpm acetate in his "custom studio." Bobby played piano and all three boys sang.

Larry kept that disc. Years later, at his request, I put it in my safe-deposit box for him. Many years after that, again at his request, I brought it back to Larry and we listened to it. The disc offered up a pretty hot medley of the boys' favorite songs of the day: "Be-Bop-A-Lula," "Earth Angel," "Ready Teddy," "In the Still of the Night," "Let the Good Times Roll," and "Lawdy Miss Clawdy."

I'm sure they weren't the only little Jewish hipsters who ever laid down a few tracks, but this particular acetate is special, to put it mildly. In the long, fabled line of Bob Dylan records, this was the first.

I have to add that Larry had talent in his own right. Along with his pal Gene LaFond, he wrote and performed songs that reflected his life, his struggles, and his eternal optimism. Here's a bit of the song, "Some Get the Chair":

There's all kinds of prisons, all kinds of jails
Somebody wins; somebody fails
In a world full of trouble, I've had my share
Some get away with murder
Some get the chair; some get the chair
This old wheelchair keeps on turning
The wheels keep spinning round and round
Just as long as there's a prayer in my heart
I won't let nothing keep me down
Can't keep me down
Can't keep me down

While he may have had his poetic side, Larry was a wild kid, always getting into trouble or stirring things up. By the time he was thirteen, he was frequently taking off in his parents' car in the middle of the night to go joyriding with friends. Bobby and I might have been a little reckless sometimes, but we didn't do anything like that. Once Larry even set off for California—though he only got as far as Iowa.

Larry's dad finally got so fed up with having to pick him up from Saint Paul Central High School for misbehaving that he enrolled Larry in military school. But underneath all his rebelliousness, Larry was a sweetheart. All the kids loved him. If he saw anyone getting picked on, he was the first to whoop the bully. He wore his heart on his sleeve and always said exactly what was on his mind. The difference between my two friends was this: If I asked Bobby and Larry the same question, Larry would answer in fifty words and Bobby would say about five—if anything at all. Bobby always came off a bit mysterious, while Larry was anything but.

One summer at Camp Herzl, Larry fell in love with a girl named Suzi. He gave her his ID bracelet, which meant they were going steady. After camp was over, he could not stop thinking about Suzi and the possibility of going "all the way" with her, so he hopped on a train to Omaha to see her.

Torrid thoughts and plans raced through Larry's mind during that nine-hour journey, but alas, he was destined for Heartbreak Hotel. When Suzi picked him up at the train station, she was accompanied by a male friend, and during Larry's entire visit, he never managed to get a moment alone with her—let alone so much as a kiss. Before he boarded the train back to Saint Paul, Suzi returned his ID bracelet, and Larry spent the entire ride home tormented by the pangs of unrequited love. He told me that when he got home, he lay on the floor of his bedroom listening to his favorite records for comfort, but the love songs just made him hurt more.

Besides being a romantic and a sensitive soul, Larry also considered himself an authority on fashion. He liked to dress well and take care of appearances—his own and others'. One weekend when I was staying at his house in

Saint Paul, I had a date with his neighbor Pam. Before-
hand, Larry went over to her house and looked through
her wardrobe to piece an outfit together for our date. He
wanted to make sure she looked good for his buddy. He
settled on a yellow crewneck, a Black Watch plaid skirt,
black knee socks, and a yellow ribbon for her ponytail. Pam
protested against the yellow sweater, but Larry insisted.
Even as a kid, he was a persuasive guy. That night, I had a
date with a beautiful girl who looked like she'd just walked
off the dance floor at *American Bandstand*.

When Larry was sixteen, tragedy struck. On a family
vacation to Miami Beach, he was with a group of kids diving into the ocean from a high retainer wall. In Minnesota,
there are ten thousand lakes but no tides, so Larry was
unaccustomed to worrying about variations in the depth
of the water. As luck would have it, the tide was out when
he took the plunge and the water was deceptively shallow.
You don't have to be a math major to figure out the consequences of diving ten feet into two feet of water: in a mere
moment, Larry was paralyzed.

By the following year, when I was thinking about
going to college and Bobby was thinking about dropping
out of college, Larry was dealing with the implications of
living out his life in a wheelchair. Though the accident
changed Larry's life forever, the bond among the three of
us remained strong.

About a week or so after the accident, Bobby and I visited Larry at the University of Minnesota Medical Center
in Minneapolis. Larry had many friends, and some of them

had told us what a heartbreaking experience it was to see him in his condition. They were right. Larry had been one of the wildest, most active kids we knew. Seeing him immobilized was surreal—like a bad dream we couldn't wake up from.

For Larry's part, he appeared to be taking it well. Mainly, he seemed annoyed, as if the whole thing were a mild inconvenience. We started joking and telling stories, and soon the three of us were laughing as usual. It seemed almost like old times. Almost.

We promised Larry we would keep in close touch, and we kept our promise. But that evening, as we walked back down the hospital corridors in silence, I saw something I'd never seen before and would never see again—Bobby with tears in his eyes.

Our friend Larry Kegan lived out his life as a quadriplegic, but he ended up accomplishing more from his wheelchair than most able-bodied people do in their entire lives. He got his masters degree in psychology and specialized in sexual therapy for handicapped people. He got married and had three great kids. He managed a facility in Guadalajara, Mexico, where handicapped people could lead full lives with dignity and minimal assistance. And he still found time to manage orange groves in Florida and occasionally join Bobby to sing at one of his sold-out gigs.

Since Larry was known as a wise spirit, people often came to him with their problems or complaints. Bobby and I loved the way Larry would handle these people, bursting forth with a veritable Sermon on the Mount from his wheelchair.

"Schmuck!" he would shout. "I can't scratch, or pick my nose, feed myself, wipe my own ass, roll over, or cook a meal. And you have the nerve to stand in front of me and complain about your life? Get out of here and go thank God for all you have. Go make this world a better place!"

FOUR

College Daze

Bobby never wanted to go to college; he wanted to focus on his music. But his parents insisted he complete his education, and out of respect for them, in the fall of 1959, he enrolled at the University of Minnesota in Minneapolis. While he may not have been gung ho about academia, he did see the move as an opportunity to leave small-town Hibbing behind and get closer to where the music was happening. Needless to say, his class attendance was spotty.

Bobby's parents were adamant that he live in the Sammy house. "Sammy" was the nickname for Sigma Alpha Mu, one of the two Jewish fraternities on campus, of which his cousin had recently been president. Though he had never been much of a joiner, the frat became Bobby's first home in Minneapolis, and he did participate in some of its activities. When the brothers wanted to put on a skit for their winter party, Bobby—along with two pledges named Bernie and Jerry—volunteered to write the script. The skit was called "Sammy Claus," and cleverly made fun of the frat brothers. Dressed in a Santa suit, Bobby played the title role and he was a big hit, playing the piano and singing while his frat brothers chugged beer and roared with laughter.

Dick, another kid we'd known at Herzl Camp, was a pledge of Sammy when Bobby was crashing there freshman year. The two of them would hang out in Bobby's little room, listening to music. Bobby was working on a mural on one of his walls. He'd used a pencil to draw a floor-to-ceiling portrait of a young guy with curly hair. Every time Dick came over, a little more had been completed. Bobby struggled with the mouth, and could never render it to his own satisfaction—so, instead, he traced his left hand two times, side by side, where the mouth should have been. He titled the piece, "The Man with Two Left Hands."

Bobby took full advantage of living in the big city, going out regularly to coffeehouses such as the Ten O'Clock Scholar and the Purple Onion. As Dick was rushing out the door to a morning class, Bobby would be coming in after a night out, guitar in hand. Biographers have reported that the Ten O'Clock Scholar was where Bobby first performed in public—but they were unaware of those rooftop gigs at Herzl Camp.

While Bobby was honing his skills in coffeehouses, I was beginning my freshman year at University of Minnesota's Duluth campus. I had enrolled there in order to stay close to the family business, where I was learning the ropes, but my sights were firmly set on transferring to Minneapolis.

In addition to my ability to box, I carried another skill to college that I'd acquired thanks to my father. To understand this story, you have to know a little about the place I grew up.

Duluth was a major port city, the westernmost port of the Great Lakes. Iron ore from the iron range—up near where Bobby lived—would be sent to Duluth via mile-long trains, and then shipped by ore boats called "lakers" to the steel mills of Pittsburgh and other cities to the east. Grain from all over the Midwest would be shipped to countries around the world in giant oceangoing vessels. The sailors and longshoremen who worked the docks adjacent to the Garfield Avenue area, where my family had its fish plant, liked to spend their after-work hours at the Tip-Top Tavern. So did my dad, and he sometimes took me along.

It was at the Tip-Top that he taught me to play cards for money. I picked up the fundamentals pretty quickly, and soon I was so proficient that I was winning my lunch money—plus plenty for other things—from the students at UMD.

Eventually, mothers began to complain to the school that some card shark was taking their kids' spending money, that they were coming home hungry and broke. As a result, card playing was banned from the student union.

Not one to be easily discouraged, I knew I had to take my games underground. Why not literally? I settled on the elevator of the student union, which I would stop between floors. Enjoying the added excitement of a clandestine game, the kids kept coming and the money kept flowing. Now, the school was receiving complaints about the non-working elevators! Eventually, the game was busted when a surprised security guard named Ollie pried the elevator door open to find me sitting on the floor surrounded by college guys, cards, and money. That was the end of my on-campus games.

I don't know what my father was thinking when he taught me how to play cards like that, but I guess he figured it was another life skill that might come in handy. All I can say is, I never had an empty pocket while I was in college.

Once a month while I was in college in Duluth, I'd go down to visit Bobby in Minneapolis. He and I would grab a bite to eat before heading over to visit Larry, who was enduring a seemingly endless cycle of surgeries. We worked hard to provide whatever encouragement and comfort we could on those visits. We'd spend most of our time talking about the good old days at Herzl Camp and speculating about the days that lay ahead. It seemed all three of us were reaching a crossroads in our lives.

Bobby couldn't wait to get out of school so he could put all of his energy into music. I wanted to leave Duluth behind and experience college life on the main campus in Minneapolis. And Larry, who was confined to a bed at that point, wanted to recover enough so that he could continue studying, chasing girls, and playing music.

Bobby often visited Larry on his own, and would bring along his guitar and entertain Larry's many visitors. His hospital room was like party central, with friends coming and going at all hours. On a number of occasions, Larry's pals would surreptitiously whisk him into a van and take him on unauthorized field trips to concerts in the park or outdoor festivals.

I'd like to say we were encouraging Larry, but in reality, it was Larry who inspired us because, despite his injuries, he never stopped moving forward.

When I was eighteen, I bought a brand-new metallic-blue 1961 Pontiac Bonneville convertible. I paid for it with money I had made working (and playing cards), added to some Bar Mitzvah money I'd squirreled away. When I was driving my friends around in that car, they would try to get me to speed and drag race with other cars on the streets—a pretty common pastime back then. I always steadfastly refused, saying, "I would rather have people say that Louie Kemp was late than refer to me as 'the late Louie Kemp.'" Larry's accident had knocked some sense into me, I guess.

By the spring of 1960, Bobby had moved out of the Sammy house and rented a small apartment above Gray's Drugstore in Dinkytown, a hip little commercial district bordering the campus and known for its coffeehouses and bohemian vibe. Dinkytown had already become Bobby's regular haunt; he found kindred spirits there who would nurture his career as a singer-songwriter. The writings of Kerouac and Ginsberg were shaping his ideas and beliefs. Nobody knew back then that he would one day become the most famous dropout since Thomas Edison.

I guess Bobby's persistence paid off, because eventually Bobby's parents gave him their blessing to drop out of college and pursue music. A deal of some sort had been negotiated in which they would help support him modestly for a while, but if the music career didn't take off, he'd have to go back to school.

With the burden of college no longer weighing him down, Bobby devoted himself full time to writing and performing. He traded in his electric guitar for an acoustic model, and sharpened his music skills by working with such talented veterans of Dinkytown as "Spider" John Koerner, Tony "Little Sun" Glover, and Dave "Snaker" Ray. It was from those guys that Bobby began to learn the skills of a folk singer, i.e., the ability to connect intimately with listeners in a way that hadn't been required for rock and roll. Rock had called for a flashy kind of stage presence, while folk singers were expected to project a kind of humility—which also served them well between sets, when passing the hat around for tips. After their gigs, Bobby and the guys would end up at one of their apartments, jamming away until the early morning hours.

Bobby continued to eat, sleep, and breathe music. He delved into the folk scene and absorbed as much as he could, becoming an avid student of folk-music history by reading everything he could find on the subject. Woody Guthrie's *Bound for Glory,* as well as the work of the Beats, became the raw material that forged him into a songwriter, performer, and thinker.

I encouraged him when I could, not that he needed it. He'd chosen an unconventional path and he knew it, but as far as I know, he never had a moment's doubt or hesitation about pursuing his dreams.

Bobby Zimmerman (center) at Herzl camp in 1957. Larry Kegan is to his left and I'm to his right. *Photo by Mark Alpert*

Bobby Zimmerman at Herzl camp in his Shabbat whites. *From the Bill Pagel Archives*

Concert poster from the Buddy Holly concert Bobby and I attended in Duluth on January 31, 1959. Buddy would die three days later in a plane crash in Iowa.

My sister Sharon and I getting our picture taken with Santa Claus at Wahl's Department Store. When I showed this photo to my five-year-old son Elie, he said, "Daddy, who is the rabbi?"

My father was very involved in the Republican party. When Eisenhower's presidential campaign tour brought him to Duluth in 1952, my sister Sharon and I presented him with a twenty-five-pound Lake Superior trout courtesy of A. Kemp Fisheries. This picture appeared in the *Duluth News Tribune* and my friends were very impressed for a day or two.

Me with my Norwegian girlfriend Lee, with whom I saw the movie *Exodus*.

THE WHITE HOUSE

WASHINGTON

February 26, 1954.

Dear Mr. Kemp:

When we returned from California on
Wednesday, we found the smoked fish
that you so kindly sent to Senator
Thye for us.   I am most appreciative
of your thoughtful courtesy.

I remember meeting you and your
children when we were in Duluth in
1952.   Please give Sharon and
Louis my best wishes, and to you
my renewed thanks.

Sincerely,

Dwight D. Eisenhower

Mr. Abe Kemp,
A. Kemp Fish Company,
105 North First Avenue East,
Duluth 2, Minnesota.

Personal

After Eisenhower got elected, my father sent him fish a few more times, via his
friend and then-Senator, Edward John Thye. This personalized letter of thanks from
the President includes a shout-out to my sister and me.

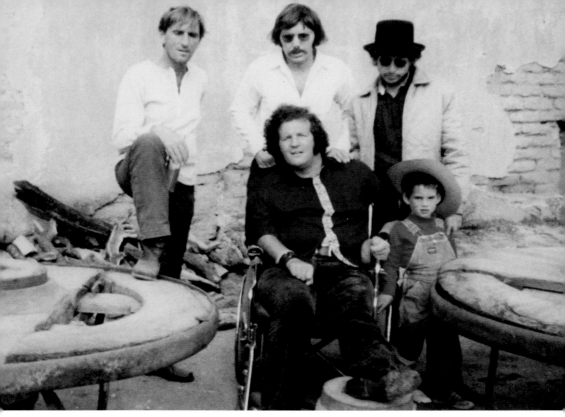

Clockwise from upper left: Harry Dean Stanton, me, Bobby, and Larry on the set of *Pat Garrett and Billy the Kid*. Bob was playing a character named Alias in the film, as well as writing the soundtrack.

My friend Stephanie and I in Las Vegas. I took Stephanie to Bob's recording session, and we were the first people to hear "Forever Young."

Above: Bob during "Tour '74."

Right: Bob on the European tour in '78.

Left to right: Bob, Levon Helm, one of the tour assistants, and Robbie Robertson. This was taken during "Tour '74," after a show, when we were all pretty tired.

During "Tour '74," pranksters Bill Graham and Barry Imhoff broke into my room and threw chickens on my bed. I didn't miss a beat, though; just continued with my business call.

Cher, Bob, and I sing "Happy Birthday" to David Geffen at the lavish surprise party thrown by Cher and Bobby, while he cuts his cake.

Marlon Brando addresses the masses at Bill Graham's 1975 benefit concert in San Francisco.

Bobby plays for the crowd.

Above: Bob and I catch a George Harrison concert in Toronto in 1974.
Photo by Arthur Usherson
Below: Bob and I with Ronnie Hawkins, after the "Tour '74" concert in
Toronto. *Photo by Arthur Usherson*

Bobby and I hanging out together in 1972.

Larry on stage singing at one of Bob's concerts while Bobby plays the saxophone. *From the Bill Pagel Archives*

I did manage to transfer over to the University of Minnesota in Minneapolis, but not before Bobby left Minneapolis entirely. I moved into the Phi Epsilon Pi fraternity house, just down the street from the Sammy house where he'd first landed. Mutual friends began asking me what the hell Bobby was doing. To them, dropping out of school and passing the hat in pizza joints to get by was like throwing away his life and future.

"Don't worry," I told them. "Bobby knows what he's doing."

And he did. The first thing he'd told me when we met at camp all those years earlier was that he was going to be a rock-and-roll star, and he never deviated from that course. In fact, he was the most determined person I'd ever met.

When Bobby moved to Dinkytown, he decided a tangible transformation was called for. He wasn't going to be Bobby Zimmerman anymore, but *Bob Dylan*. He had been telling people for a long time that he was going to go east, and now he was ready to do it.

One winter morning, he headed out on foot toward the entrance of Interstate 35W with his guitar over his shoulder, a small suitcase, and five dollars in his sock. As he stuck his thumb out to hitchhike, the snow was coming down so hard that he had to keep shaking himself off so people would know he was real and not a snowman.

When a guy finally pulled over and asked him where he was headed, Bob yelled, "New York City!"

"I'm just going as far as Madison," the man said, "but if you want to come with, jump in!"

Bob was thrilled to be out of the blizzard, in a warm car, and on his way somewhere. He wasn't about to quibble about the destination. He ended up staying in Madison for a while, and then Chicago, hanging out and making money playing in the coffeehouses—but he hadn't lost sight of his goal of moving to New York, meeting Woody Guthrie, and expanding his horizons.

Eventually, he got back on the road and scored a ride as far as the other side of the George Washington Bridge. He soon found his way to Greenwich Village and started his climb to stardom—all while I was chilling (literally) on the UM campus.

From the time I was around thirteen, I was a champion arm-wrestler, able to beat everyone my age—even the football players and weight lifters—as well as many of my teachers and counselors. One day I was in the process of arm-wrestling the whole fraternity one after another, usually slamming their arms down in seconds. One of my frat brothers, a great guy named Paul Goldstein, saw that I was mowing through the guys and decided he wanted to show me up. He went and found his friend Carl Eller, the All-American defensive end for the Golden Gophers, who later became an All-Pro star for the Vikings and an NFL Hall of Famer. Because of his size and strength, everybody called Carl "Moose."

Paul invited Moose to come over and destroy me, and I guess the guy figured it would be a fun piece of cake. When I looked up to see how many more victims lay ahead of me, I was astonished to see Moose in line about seven guys back. He had his arms crossed over his chest and stared grimly in my direction—which made me break out in a big smile.

"Let's see how good you are now, big shot," Paul cackled.

Moose waited his turn. When he got to the front of the line and sat down across from me, I had to admit he was pretty intimidating. His hand looked more like a club, and when he locked it with mine, my elbow dangled six inches off the table. I had never seen an arm as big as his. Gamely, I called for someone to bring over some phone books and I put them under my elbow to get some leverage. Then we got to it, each of us trying hard to conquer the other. My frat brothers were all screaming and yelling, some for me, and some chanting, "Moose! Moose! Moose!"

Bets were thrown, and anyone betting on me got big odds. It was brother against brother, just like in Civil War times, and the profanities were flying. Our arms wavered back and forth, a couple of inches each way, as the veins in our necks popped and our faces turned beet red. We huffed and puffed, groaned and moaned, and after about five minutes—which is a long time in arm-wrestling—it seemed obvious that neither of us was going to fold. We mutually decided to call it a draw, to the amazement of the crowd.

After that epic showdown, whenever I saw Carl on campus, he came over and shook my hand. "You are one tough Jew boy," he'd say—which was a big compliment coming from the Moose.

After a particularly cold day on campus, when the windchill had brought the temperature down to around minus thirty, I decided that, as long as I'd left home to go to college, I might as well go someplace warm. Back at the frat house, I got out a map and jabbed my finger at a spot about as far south as I could without going into the ocean.

Miami.

I went to the library and looked up University of Miami, got the phone number, and called the admissions office. The guy on the other end of the phone was friendly, receptive, and encouraging.

"Oh, yeah," he said, "if you go to University of Minnesota, you won't have any trouble getting in here. Just have them send your transcripts to me. I'll take care of you."

"OK," I replied, "and by the way, what's the temperature down there?"

"Oh, about eighty today," he said. "I'm going to the beach in a little while to grab some rays."

That sealed the deal for me. I made arrangements to transfer there for spring quarter. It turned out that there was a branch of our Phi Ep fraternity on campus, so I asked the president of our chapter to call down and let them know I was coming. It worked out, and I was all set up with a place to stay among my new frat brothers. When the time came, I packed up my Corvette and drove all the way to the Sunshine State with barely a stop along the way.

The frat house was a great landing place, but the following year I moved into an apartment in Coconut Grove with one of the guys. It was a good life down there, near the beach, and we'd make frequent trips to watch jai alai and bet on our favorite players. The girls were great, too—and you could actually see them, since they weren't all bundled up like they were back in Minnesota.

My friends up north were shocked when I made the move—but they were more than happy to come visit me during spring break. We'd head up to Fort Lauderdale and have some crazy times with all the other college kids. I ended up leaving Miami before I graduated, though. Just before my final quarter, my father got sick and I had to drop out so I could help him with the family fish business.

Two years later, Dad passed away and I took over the business. It was daunting, and maybe not exactly how I'd expected it all to go down, but I managed to transition successfully into the next phase of my life. There were times I missed the freedom I'd had in college and the frivolity of it all. But I recognized my responsibility—and the opportunity the business presented—and I wholeheartedly embraced what my father had groomed me for.

FIVE

Rising Stars

What happens when your closest friend from childhood becomes one of the most famous people in the world, seemingly overnight? What effect does being apart for ten years have on a friendship? Sometimes, these momentous changes have no effect at all.

It may sound kind of crazy, but Bob and I were sometimes the closest when we were the farthest apart. We saw each other from the inside out, not from the outside in, like everyone else did. We had a covenant that seemed to defy time and geography.

While Bob was struggling to make it in New York, I was busy running my father's business. Whatever news I got about him during those years came from his mom, Beatty. According to her, he was getting by as a musician, still pursuing his dream.

Then, one day, Beatty told me that "her Bobby" had just played Carnegie Hall!

A rush of pride washed over me. It was not too long after that when Bob started to get some press. He wasn't yet a star, but he was definitely on the rise, and it was an exciting thing to watch, even from afar.

Growing up in Hibbing, a blue-collar mining town, had surely had an impact on Bob. The people there worked hard and often made a decent wage, but there weren't a lot of possibilities for growth or advancement. Perhaps what had made an even greater impact on his worldview was his Jewish upbringing. Every Jewish kid celebrating Passover knew the story of our people's enslavement in Egypt. During Hanukkah, we lit our menorahs in commemoration of our ancestors, the Maccabees, and their fight for religious freedom. We were taught about the Spanish Inquisition and the pogroms in Eastern Europe that accounted for many of our grandparents' escape to America.

As teenagers, we were struck by the reality of what had occurred not much more than a decade earlier in Europe—the Holocaust. In 1960, the movie *Exodus*, starring Paul Newman as a brave member of the Haganah attempting to lead a group of his people to freedom in Palestine, was released. I remember coming out of the Granada Theater on Superior Street, in downtown Duluth, furious. In a rage, I began pounding on a parking meter as my girlfriend, a Norwegian girl named Lee, tried to calm me down.

"Louie," she said, "it's just a movie."

It was not just a movie to me. The injustices done to these poor survivors sickened me. It sickened many of us. Supporting the underdog is virtually second nature to Jews because we have so often been in that position ourselves. We seem to have a sixth sense when it comes to persecution, discrimination, and injustice, and many of us have devoted our lives to battling these things. There's no question in my mind that Bob's drive to write songs that mattered was born at least in part from his roots as a Jew.

On August 28, 1963, along with millions of other people around the world, I watched Martin Luther King, Jr., deliver his "I Have a Dream" speech at his historic March on Washington. Only Beatty Zimmerman could have been prouder than I was as Bob sang "When the Ship Comes In" with Joan Baez, and his solo version of "Only a Pawn in Their Game." Then Peter, Paul and Mary sang a song of Bob's that had been released just three months earlier, that was destined to become an anthem of the civil rights movement. That song was "Blowin' in the Wind."

Bobby was only twenty-two years old at the time. Just four and a half years had passed since the two of us had seen Buddy Holly play in Duluth. In the interim, *Bobby* had become *Bob* and had started changing the world. I had built up a very successful fish business. Not bad for two small-town dropouts! I can only imagine what we might have accomplished if we'd paid more attention to our studies.

Those years marked the longest period of time that Bob and I were ever physically separated. Throughout that time, we relied on Beatty to keep us informed of each other's activities. Thus, we were never completely out of touch. Today, looking back from the vantage point of having had an all-access pass to Bob's life for fifty years, I guess I knew he would reach out to me when he was ready.

I also knew this was a seminal time for Bob. He'd broken onto the scene at Café Wha? in Greenwich Village, playing harmonica for a dollar a day plus a cheeseburger.

(He often gave his french fries to Tiny Tim.) Soon he was opening for John Lee Hooker at Gerde's Folk City, and soon after that, he was signed by Columbia Records. When Joan Baez showcased him in her concerts, it propelled him to fame in the folk world. When he went electric at the Newport Folk Festival in 1965, it turned up the temperature even higher.

Somehow, within the cauldron of the sixties, Bob found time to get married, have kids, become a major star in his own right, survive a motorcycle accident, appear on the cover of *Rolling Stone,* and write songs that not only sold millions, but went on to become the soundtrack of our lives.

Through Beatty, Bob apparently followed my exploits almost as closely as I monitored his. At one point, I made an extremely lucrative deal to expand our fish business up into Alaska. The ink was barely dry on the contracts when Beatty called.

"Bobby says congratulations, Louie!" she told me. "He said to say he's proud of ya!"

"That," I replied, "is exactly how I feel about him."

It was true. Whenever I heard that Peter, Paul and Mary version of "Blowin' in the Wind," I felt a wave of vicarious satisfaction. *Wow! Good for Bobby!* I thought, as he broke down the doors and smashed the windows of the outdated musical, cultural, and political establishment. He was playing on the world stage in every respect, while I was doing my thing in a more conventional way. Yet, it was not entirely surprising to watch my childhood friend grow into *the* Bob Dylan. He'd been creating and nurturing that transformation from the earliest childhood experiences we'd shared.

So, as millions of people began to figure out who had written "Blowin' in the Wind," and become fans of everything he did, my emotions about my friend went far deeper than mere pride or vicarious excitement. What I felt was vindication. I thought of all the kids who'd laughed at Bobby, all the squares who hadn't gotten what he was doing, all the adults who'd been offended by his raucous, singular music.

Over the years, old friends have confessed to me that they felt embarrassed about how they'd unceremoniously thrown Bobby, Larry, and me out of those long-ago open houses. I just laugh.

Vindication.

And if anyone thinks *vindication* is an odd attitude to lead with after all these years, perhaps it's because they haven't shared Bobby's dream as long as I have. I believe that's why I'm the only person from his past that he has ever reached out to and reunited with in a meaningful way.

When it comes down to it, our friendship has never had anything to do with music or fish. For years, I shared his hopes and disappointments, his triumphs and difficulties. Sometimes I think I even dreamed his dreams with him. Those dreams were like a fixed point in an ever-changing world.

To the world, Bob Dylan came onto the scene like a shooting star. He was a man of mystery, a modern-day rock-and-roll prophet. To me, he was an old pal. Restless.

Eccentric. Mischievous to the core, yet a serious soul who nobody had taken seriously for a long, long time. When I think about Bobby, I think about those blue eyes sparkling with chutzpah. I think about how he always dared to be different but remained fiercely loyal over all those years, in his own way.

To me, Bob Dylan is still Bobby Zimmerman. Still the kid on the roof. Still my blood brother.

SIX

MacDougal Street to Durango

One of the main happening spots in daytime Duluth was the Glass Block Department Store on Superior Street. Glass Block was where you did a little shopping for clothes, then sat for coffee or a milkshake and a quick bite in the café before continuing on with your day. I guess you could call it the Neiman Marcus of Duluth.

It was in the summer of 1972 in downtown Duluth, right near the Glass Block, that I ran into Beatty. We hugged each other, and as I looked into her eyes, I realized that the two of us were part of a rapidly dwindling group of people who still called Bob *Bobby*.

"He asks about you a lot," Beatty said. "If you ever get to New York, he'd like to get together with you."

"He must have been reading my mail," I said, "or my mind. I'm going to New York in a month!"

She asked for my current phone number, and a few days later, she called to say that Bobby wanted me to call him as soon as I got to the city. Then she gave me his number.

About a month later, I checked into the Park Lane Hotel across from Central Park. First thing I did, even before I unpacked, was call Bobby.

After a couple of rings, he picked up, his voice sounding the same as always. He seemed happy to hear from me. He said he was living on MacDougal Street, down in the Village, and gave me the address.

"I'll meet you in the little café across the street from my place," he said.

An hour later, we were sitting across from each other at a rickety table in that little café. It was just like old times.

By that point, Bobby had been married to Sara for about seven years and had five kids. Being a family man looked good on him—but it really brought home just how long we had been apart. He had a wife and kids, but he was relaxed and happy. Seeing my old friend, whom I hadn't seen in over a decade, in a state like that made me happy, too. Bobby seemed to be relishing this time out of the spotlight.

I told him the news from Minnesota and all about my new girlfriend. He shared some of the experiences he'd had since he'd hitchhiked to New York disguised as a snowman. The timing of his arrival had apparently been excellent. Greenwich Village in 1961 was spitting out energy like a well-oiled chainsaw, and it did not take him long to make inroads among the prominent hipsters of the day. Having situated himself within the beating heart of the folk-music scene, he rustled up gigs at local clubs, met creative musicians and interesting women, and—more important than any of that—wrote songs like a demon in the night.

Within eight months of getting there, Bobby had been officially "discovered." He chuckled to himself as he told me about it.

"It was a few blocks from here," he said, gesturing casually down MacDougal Street like a guy hailing a slow-moving taxi, "at a place called Gerde's Folk City."

As he told it, there was an older, distinguished-looking guy in the front row who stood out because he was wearing a suit and tie. Somebody told him it was John Hammond, who, according to Bobby, was a legendary, visionary producer at Columbia Records.

"He discovered everybody worth discovering," Bobby explained. The list included Billie Holiday, Benny Goodman, Count Basie, Robert Johnson, Bessie Smith, Aretha Franklin, Pete Seeger, Stevie Ray Vaughan, and Bruce Springsteen. (Those last two came along later, of course.) Anyway, it was that night that Hammond discovered a twenty-year-old from Hibbing, Minnesota, named Bob Dylan.

Hammond caught a fair amount of shit for signing Bobby. Some of the other suits at Columbia openly joked that Hammond had lost it, snidely referring to Bobby as "Hammond's Folly." These must have been the same guys who'd picked Barabbas over Jesus and buried Mozart in a pauper's grave. They would soon be forced to realize the error of their ways.

After we'd sat at the café for a couple of hours and exhausted our best stories, Bobby took me across MacDougal to meet his wife and kids before they headed out to the Hamptons for the weekend. Beatty had already told me a little bit about Sara, exulting in the fact that her Bobby had settled down with a nice Jewish girl who was proving herself to be a devoted wife and a wonderful mother. Apparently, Bobby and Sara had met through Sara's friend Sally Buchler, who had been dating Bobby's manager, Albert Grossman.

I immediately sensed a quiet confidence in Sara. Her curiosity about our childhood adventures seemed genuine, and the flow of our conversation, natural. And, while it was very obvious in the way she spoke that she was well read and intelligent, Sara lacked all pretension. She was a classy lady and absolutely stunning, but there was also something very *hamish*—homey—about her. And, maybe because of that, their apartment truly felt warm and inviting. Lived in. Sara offered us drinks and things to nibble on as their five young kids, a couple of them still toddlers, stumbled in and out of the room, laughing and entertaining themselves.

Bobby wore his fame lightly. I remember thinking that he seemed to be leading the simple, happy life of a typical northern Minnesota boy, except that people kept trying to put crowns on his head. "Messiah," some called him. "The Voice of His Generation." He took it all in stride, like the tissue of horseshit it was.

Most tourists head straight for the Empire State Building or Statue of Liberty, but Bobby showed me a very different kind of attraction. As we sat in the apartment building's small courtyard, Bobby gestured toward the fence, through which we could see the building's garbage cans. They had apparently become famous along with Bobby; people rifled through them regularly, he told me, to find out more about the mysterious Bob Dylan.

When I realized he wasn't joking, I said, "Well … I guess that means you've arrived!"

Bobby laughed, but there was a strange expression on his face—part resignation, part irritation. But I could swear I saw a glimmer of pride there too.

Without a word, Bobby got up and disappeared. A moment later, there he was, on the other side of the fence, backing up his station wagon. He called out that he wanted to show me something. Knowing him for the mischievous and mysterious creature he was, this set off a little warning bell in my brain, but he was gunning the engine impatiently—so I raced out to join him, and off we went.

Bobby was a good driver, if a bit impulsive, which served him well on the streets of New York. I tried to get him to reveal our destination but he steadfastly refused. My anticipation intensified as we crossed a massive bridge and at last arrived in the magical kingdom of Brooklyn.

Bobby had taken us to Williamsburg, which resembled an Eastern European shtetl more than a New York City neighborhood. All of the signs in the shop windows were in Yiddish or Hebrew: the pharmacies, the hardware stores, and, of course, the delis. Thousands of Orthodox Jewish men strolled the streets in their traditional black hats and coats. The women, modestly dressed, pushed double strollers followed by a flock of children. I'd had no clue that a place like this existed, certainly not in a major metropolitan city like New York.

We drove around taking it all in, then headed back to Manhattan, chatting about what we'd seen and about old times. As the memories came back, I could see the old mischief returning to Bobby's eyes. He'd been nudging me with questions about my girlfriend in Minneapolis, and now suggested that we give her a call.

Keep in mind that prank phone calls had been a part of our MO as teenage troublemakers. And, although we were grown men now, with careers and commitments, we'd both retained our fundamentally juvenile sense of humor. What some might call childish behavior, the two of us still found funny as hell. So, the minute we got back to Bobby's place, I called my girl in Minneapolis.

We hadn't done much more than exchange hellos before Bobby began signaling to me to let him talk to her.

"Say hello to my friend Ricky," I told my girlfriend.

"OK," she said, and I handed the phone to Bobby.

"Ricky" had barely started to talk to her when we both started giggling.

"How old are you?" Bobby inquired.

"Twenty-one," she answered, truthfully. (I told you I was young at heart!)

"Have you ever stopped to think that you may be a little too old for Louie?"

I let out a laugh and fought for the phone, but Bobby kept a tight grip on the receiver and rolled on relentlessly.

"He only has about a couple million bucks," he told her. "I'm not sure he can support you."

"Let me speak to Louie," I could hear her shout into the phone, but Bobby was on a roll and he went on teasing her until she hung up in exasperation.

The next morning, Bobby had to head out to the Hamptons to meet up with Sara and the kids. He asked if I wanted to come along, and, seeing as I had a few days off and was having such a great time with my old pal, I accepted his invitation. We left by train that evening, and a few hours and couple dozen stops later, got off at a little train station on Long Island—a world away from Mac-Dougal Street.

No need for a taxi, Bobby told me; we could walk to the house. After what seemed like miles of trekking through dark streets, the silence broken occasionally by a dog barking in the distance, I asked if we were almost there.

"Yeah, it's not far now," he said. Bobby was a brisk walker and in good shape, and he seemed to be enjoying testing my endurance.

On we went.

"How far is it?" I asked breathlessly after ten more minutes of torture.

"Not far," he said again, laughing delightedly at my distress. The man still enjoyed pulling a little prank on me.

Eventually, we did make it to the house that I had begun to doubt even existed, and it was a perfect refuge from the big city. Over the next few days, we took long walks up and down the pristine beach, breathing in the fresh, salty air. We read, relaxed, and watched the kids play in the dunes. Sara was quite the cook, and each night the kitchen counter was laden with heaping dishes of local seafood, fresh fruit, salads, and sweets.

In my early thirties and still a bachelor, I suddenly found

getting married and having kids to be very much on my mind. I guess it was a result of hanging out with Bobby and the family, watching his kids play and run free.

"Being a father must be the best thing there is," I said to him at one point.

"It really is the best," he said, nodding.

We returned to New York after a few days in the Hamptons, and Bobby once again played tour guide. We walked around Greenwich Village and he pointed out a few places where he used to hang out. As we walked past an old theater, Sara teased Bobby.

"Your friend Neil Diamond is playing here right now," she said, pointing up at the marquee.

He smiled cryptically and motioned for us to keep on walking.

Back in Minnesota, my soon-to-be ex-girlfriend picked me up at the airport in the car I'd lent her.

"How'd you like talking to my friend Ricky?" I asked.

"He was OK," she mumbled. "Typical New York wise guy, I guess."

"Millions of people might disagree with you," I said. "That was Bob Dylan."

"What?!"

I guess I wasn't prepared for how mad she'd get at our little prank. I had embarrassed her, she insisted. I had *mortified* her.

After that night, I never saw her again. Looking back, I'm not particularly proud of the effect our little phone prank had on a perfectly sweet girl. But I do cherish the memory because it was then that I knew Bobby and I were still our old selves. Any lingering doubts that we might have grown apart over the years vanished as we laughed and struggled over that phone. And, in those few days with his family in the Hamptons, we filled in any gaps that might have opened as we'd pursued our separate dreams. I remember thinking how remarkable it was that two adults who hadn't seen each other in over a decade could still be so close and easily fall into the playful patterns of the past. And not just any two people; one of us was Bob Dylan.

Though fame had changed the way others looked at Bobby, he had not really changed. I'd enjoyed the time I'd spent with him in New York, and I'm pretty sure he came away from it knowing that I would always be somebody he could trust and confide in, someone who didn't want anything from him.

Just before I left for Minnesota, Bobby had asked me if I'd like to join him on a movie set in Mexico. I'd asked if maybe our good friend Larry could join, and Bobby had said sure, that'd be nice.

So, one cold February morning, I gladly departed Minnesota yet again, this time for Mexico, where I was picked up by Larry and his Mexican assistant, Alfonso. Both of them had lived in Mexico for years and knew more about it than anyone on any Hollywood movie set. Soon we were skimming our way across the desert in Larry's trusted van, on the dusty road to Durango.

The film *Pat Garrett and Billy the Kid* was being shot on location by Sam Peckinpah, who was known as an artsy, blood-and-guts director. Kris Kristofferson was playing Billy the Kid, James Coburn was playing Pat Garrett, and Bobby was playing a quirky character named Alias. He was also writing the soundtrack.

Being on a movie set alternates between real excitement and something akin to watching grass grow. I knew Bobby had deliberately waited until things were beginning to wrap up so he'd have some time to spend with us, and it worked out perfectly. I also knew that he'd been working and playing a lot with Kristofferson, so I asked him what he thought of his music.

"A lot of big music acts really have nothing to say," Bobby said. "Guys like Kris, Leon [Russell], and Kinky [Friedman] have a lot to say. They should say it. And they don't need makeup and dry ice."

Late one night, after everyone had left the set, Bobby sat on a tree stump strumming his guitar while I reclined in the director's chair. He asked if I'd like to hear a few songs that he'd written for the soundtrack, and—of course—I was eager to hear them.

In the fickle world of film, a song from the soundtrack can occasionally outperform the movie itself. Just think of "Moon River"—composed by Henry Mancini for *Breakfast at Tiffany's*—or Elvis Presley's "Viva Las Vegas." It was about to happen again, but nobody, except possibly Bobby, knew it at the time.

I was pleased to be among the very first to hear the songs.

"That one is pretty good," I said, taking pains to keep my comments sober, brief, and free of bullshit.

"You think?" he said, breaking into a grin.

In case you're wondering, the song was, "Knockin' on Heaven's Door."

Bobby seemed to be having a good old time on the set. He had become friendly with the great character actor Harry Dean Stanton, who was very talented and a lot of fun to hang with. When he wasn't working, Harry liked to sing and drink and drink and sing. So did Bobby. For that matter, so did Larry. I was the only one who stayed sober, so it was on me to make sure nobody got in any trouble.

When the filming was over, we decided we'd travel through Mexico for a while, so Larry, Bobby, Harry Dean, and I hopped in Larry's van and took off for Mazatlán. We stayed at a funky little hotel on the beach, where my three amigos jammed together and drank tequila, and I drank a hell of a lot of orange juice.

At one point, Larry asked Bobby to sing one of his well-known songs; I can't remember which one. To my surprise—because who could deny Larry anything?—Bobby said no. I guess I kind of lost it.

"Don't give us that 'BOB DYLAN' SHIT," I yelled. "Your friend just asked you to sing a song, Bobby Zimmerman, so JUST SING IT!"

When he refused again, I jumped onto the bed where

he was sitting and started to wrestle with him, while Larry and Harry yelled at us to stop. "Sing … him … the damn … song," I grunted as we tussled around, until finally we all just burst out laughing. It was all good—just like old times.

After a few days, Bobby was starting to get recognized. For my part, I was amazed that the three of them could still recognize *each other*. We hopped in Larry's trusty van and headed over to Guadalajara, where Larry had lived for a long time and run a facility for the disabled. We met a lot of friendly Mexicans, none of whom had ever heard of Bob Dylan but all of whom knew and loved Larry.

Larry was enjoying being the star for a change. Bobby was relieved to be anonymous, and Harry Dean was feeling no pain. It was past time for me to get back to my fish business, so I found an airport and left the three of them to drive north. They ended up stopping for a few days at Leon Russell's house before going on to Minneapolis.

SEVEN

"Tour '74"

In the fall of 1973, Bobby was recording an album that would eventually be called *Planet Waves* at the Village Studio in Santa Monica, California. He had recently signed with David Geffen's new label, Asylum Records, and had told me to drop by the studio any time.

This was a busy time for me: it was our fish company's first season in Western Alaska, harvesting and processing salmon from the Kuskokwim Delta, which is closer to the Russian line than to Anchorage. I had an Eskimo girl-friend, Natasha, who was a far cry from the nice Jewish girl my mother had always insisted I bring home. I solved the problem by not going home at all. Instead I went to Los Angeles to hang out with Bobby.

One day, I showed up at the studio with another girl I knew, Stephanie. Steph was a real stunner: a tall blonde with sparkling blue eyes, highly skilled in the smart-ass department. We had met at a leather store in San Francisco's North Beach neighborhood, where she worked as a designer, crafting amazing pieces out of suede and leather. Not only did I walk out of the store with a few great jackets, I also walked out with Steph.

A few weeks later, Steph visited me in L.A., and I thought it would be fun to take her to meet Bobby. We found him in the midst of a creative quandary. He had recorded two very different versions of the same song, and he'd been wrestling with which one to use on the record. He hadn't played the song for anyone yet, so it was by chance that Stephanie and I became the first people to hear "Forever Young."

"Bob," said Stephanie after he finished playing both versions for us, "you're getting mushy in your old age."

I waited to see how Bobby would respond to this rather flippant critique by a girl he'd just met. He looked at her somberly. Then he laughed.

"And what do you think, Louie?" he asked.

"I don't know which version you should use," I said, "but I think it's one of the best songs you've ever written."

I couldn't possibly have known it then, but that song takes on more meaning for me with every tomorrow I live. I imagine it speaks to almost everyone at some point in his or her life—whether it's the birth of children, the passing of parents, or just the feeling of getting older.

Bobby was hanging around with David Geffen quite a bit. One night, after a particularly grueling recording session, Geffen invited the two of us over to his house in Holmby Hills, where Joni Mitchell happened to be staying. Geffen was managing her at the time, and she was recording for his label.

We settled down in a magnificent room full of antique furniture and dark-paneled wooden walls. Bobby and Joni got absorbed in talking shop; she had just finished recording *Court and Spark* and he was up to his eyeballs in *Planet Waves*. After a while, Joni offered to play us a few of the songs from the new album.

Bobby and I sat on a colorful plush couch opposite Joni. She was absolutely beautiful, and I'll never forget her infectious smile, her playfulness, and her charm. She exuded a kind of quiet confidence, and her soothing, melancholy voice absolutely mesmerized me.

Believe it or not, while Joni sang, Bobby fell asleep. I don't mean he nodded out for a few seconds; I literally had to shake him to wake him up! Maybe it sounds funny now, but at the time, I was pretty embarrassed for him.

"We've been staying up late," I explained, "and he's been working really hard on his album!"

My excuses sounded like bullshit, even to me, but Joni took it all gracefully.

"At least he didn't snore," she said, then giggled.

Right about then, Geffen walked in.

"What'd you think of Joni's new songs?" he asked.

I'm sure he thought we were high when we all burst out laughing.

A few days later, Bobby told me he'd been invited by Geffen to go to Las Vegas—did I want to go with him?

Of course I did.

Soon, the two of us were flying to the desert to meet Geffen at the Sahara Hotel and Casino, where Sonny and Cher were performing. Before the curtain went up, we made our way backstage. We could tell immediately that something was wrong with this picture. The entourage seemed to be divided into two warring camps, and each side was ignoring the other. On one side stood Sonny, surrounded by a gaggle of attractive young women. On the other stood Cher; her assistant; her sister, Georganne; and Geffen.

At the time, Sonny and Cher had a monster-hit TV show on which they sang and bantered like a loving, bickering married couple, and everybody—including me—thought they were happy together. When I saw Cher hugging and cuddling with Geffen, I was confused.

"She's married to Sonny," I whispered to Bobby. "What gives?"

"Oh, they're separated," he told me, as if he were explaining the facts of life to a six-year-old. "Cher and David are dating."

As we took our seats for the show, Bobby was still laughing at my naïveté. All I could think about during the set was that an entertainer's life really is a performance on all fronts. I understood that, more than a couple, Sonny and Cher were a *business*—and keeping up appearances had to be part of the plan.

After the show, we all got together for a late dinner: Cher, David, Bobby, Georganne, Cher's assistant, and me. Whatever tension I had felt backstage was gone, and Cher and David lit up the entire table with their electric chemistry. We passed the time crammed into a little booth, laughing, drinking, and enjoying one another until almost sunrise.

The next day, Bobby and I and my shattered innocence flew back to L.A.

Not long after our Vegas trip, Bobby invited me to join him on a national tour, his first in seven years. It was going to be called, simply, "Tour '74," and he was going to be backed by The Band—in my opinion, the most original and authentic group in America. And I wasn't alone in that; they were more famous than even Bobby's garbage cans at the time.

"Tour '74" promised to be a major cultural event, and I credit Geffen for making it happen. He masterminded the whole thing, bringing in Bill Graham to produce and promote, and scheduling it to coincide with the release of *Planet Waves.* After that, it was up to Bobby and the Band to make history—and they did.

I had gone back to Duluth, where our fish company was in the midst of Lake Superior herring and lutefisk season. Bobby had told me very little about "Tour '74," and I wasn't sure if he was being mysterious or just didn't know much about it himself. All I remembered was the last thing he'd told me before I'd left Los Angeles for Duluth: "I'll see you after you take care of your fish. Meet me at the house in Malibu on the morning of January 1. We'll leave for the tour from there."

On the appointed date, I arrived at Bobby's house in Malibu, which he'd moved into after filming the movie in Mexico. I knew very little about the journey I was embarking on. How were we traveling? How long would we be on the road? What role was I to play, if any? I decided to just go along with things; that all would become clear soon enough.

I visited with Bobby, Sara, and the kids for a few hours, and then a limo pulled into the driveway. Without any drama, Bobby said good-bye to his family and turned to walk out the door.

Before I could follow him, Sara pulled me aside and said, "Louie, take good care of him."

The look in her eyes said it all: *Keep Bobby company; be his trusted friend; watch over him.* These were all things I was happy and qualified to do.

We arrived at a small airport. The limo drove right onto the tarmac and pulled up next to a private jet. Doors were opened, and Bill Graham and his business partner, Barry Imhoff, greeted and fussed over Bobby.

"This is my friend, Louie," Bobby said as I got out of the car. "He'll be coming along on the tour."

Bill and Barry appeared blindsided. Clearly, Bobby had neglected to mention me until that moment. I could just hear them thinking, *Who is this Louie guy? How does he fit in?* I'd been on the tour for less than five minutes and already I was causing problems. Hotel reservations had been made, and there weren't any for me. The first stop on the tour was Chicago and the Ritz-Carlton was fully booked. What to do?

"No problem," Bobby said. "Louie can stay in my room." I ended up sleeping on the couch in Bobby's suite, and it turned out that a couch at the Ritz-Carlton was more comfortable than a bed anywhere else in the world. After

Chicago, arrangements were made for me to have my own room.

A large private jet had been chartered for the tour, and it had been reconfigured into an upscale flying condominium, featuring beds, comfy chairs, and every amenity imaginable. It was as close to having a home as you could get on the road, and Bobby, the members of the Band, and I took full advantage of it. Sometimes Graham and Geffen joined us. Bob, the guys from The Band, and I all traveled together between the hotels and concert venues in a special camper.

Once Graham figured out I was there to stay, he gave me the best seat in the house at every concert. Actually, it wasn't a seat at all; it was an ornate, extremely comfortable rocking chair that he had placed onstage before each gig, so close to Levon Helm that I could almost reach out and touch him. Levon once told me that, as the drummer, he always had the best seat in the house, because the audience was where the real show was. I found out firsthand that he was right.

Never was that more vivid to me than on this one night when Bobby and all the musicians had left the stage and were waiting to return for the encore. There I sat, on the stage alone in my rocking chair, letting the roaring ocean of applause and cheers wash over me in waves. One by one, little flickers of light began to appear in the dark sea, as one after another fan ignited a lighter and held it high in the air. Nowadays, that's pretty standard—and the light comes from cell phones—but I believe I was the first "layperson" to see that amazing sight from the stage. I quickly ran into the wings, found Bobby, and told him, "You have to come out and see this!"

He followed me to a spot where we could peep out at the vast audience and, as promised, the sight was majestic—like a million stars shining from the heavens.

The two boys from the North Country looked at each other as if to say, *Where else could we possibly want to be?*

"Tour '74" was like living in a bubble. As we flew in our luxurious private jet from city to city, we had a legion of people looking out for us. We stayed in first-class hotels, traveled in fancy vehicles to big arenas. Security was tight, and when we got hungry, there was always room service.

Every night after the show, Bobby and I ate dinner in his room. We were always ravenous, so while we waited for room service to knock on the door, we often talked about food. We both agreed we wanted to eat healthier. Bobby said that after he ate a steak he always felt tired. "Besides," he said, "it makes your digestive system work harder." So, one night at the Plaza Hotel in New York City, we made a pact never to eat red meat again. For the rest of the tour, we didn't touch the stuff.

Some months later, Bobby and I went out to dinner in Los Angeles. When the waitress came over, Bobby ordered a steak.

"Bobby!" I said. "Steak?"

"They have great steaks here," he replied.

"But … we agreed we weren't going to eat any more red meat!"

"Are you still doing that?" he asked, looking genuinely perplexed.

It's been about forty-five years, and I still don't eat red meat. As for Bobby, well …

Being on the road can be a beautiful and exciting experience. This is true whether you're staying at the Ritz or a Motel 6. I never did get used to the feeling of being swarmed by a cheering crowd though, just because I was a member of Bobby's entourage. It was like I was being cheered for sticking with my childhood friend.

One thing I did get used to was the fact that when you're a friend of a star, you meet a lot of other stars in the same constellation. Over the course of "Tour '74," I had gotten to know the guys in The Band pretty well. They were special people and very accomplished musicians, true gems who shined brightly. Bobby couldn't have chosen his touring companions more wisely.

I also got to know Bill Graham and Barry Imhoff pretty well. They were professionals and took a lot of pride in their work. Graham could be tough, but he was a real mensch, always making sure everyone was OK and had what they needed. In San Francisco, he even tried to play matchmaker for me, introducing me to a beautiful girl named Kitty. She was smart and witty and we had a good time together. When I saw Bill later in L.A., he asked me about her and I told him what a nice girl she was, and that we planned on keeping in touch.

Graham patted me on the back.

"Good, Louie," he said. "She's a special girl and she's had a difficult life. She needs to be around good people. Y'know, she's Lenny Bruce's daughter."

Who knew?

One of the great things about touring is that you never know who you're going to meet. In my normal, day-to-day life in those days, the people I came in contact with were less diverse. Conversations tended to revolve around fish, the seasons, boats, bills—business stuff. I had to make sure I was always ahead of the competition, always growing the company. By 1974, I was up to 150 employees who relied on me to make sure their jobs were secure so they could take care of their families. I loved my work and my company, but the pressure was enormous. Going on tour allowed me to let my hair down a little. It was a change of pace and a change of scenery, to say the least.

My business was never far from my mind though. Whenever I had a chance, I'd find a phone and dial up Alaska, Duluth, or Japan to check in, make decisions, or sort out conflicts. In addition to all those employees, I was buying salmon from five hundred Inuit fishermen in Alaska and bringing in millions of pounds of fish from Lake Superior. And this was in the days before mobile technology. I took and made calls from pay phones in hotel lobbies, hotel rooms, restaurant offices, backstage at concert venues—anywhere I could find a free line. A couple of times I was on a call in an airport lobby while Bobby and the guys waited on the tarmac, ready to take off. They were good sports though. They never left without me.

Although being on tour was like a working vacation for me, I still managed to relax and enjoy myself a little. In most of the cities we visited, there was some time to walk around and see the sights, or just take leisurely walks with no destination in mind. We'd pass the day checking out museums or sitting in cafés before hustling back for sound check and showtime.

Traveling around also gave me an opportunity to catch up with friends I hadn't seen in years. In Miami, I took Bobby to Coconut Grove, where we met up with an old frat brother of mine. He took us for a long walk through the streets, which were dotted with colorful old-style Bahamian houses and the lush foliage of manicured gardens. The ritzy hotel we stayed at was a far cry from the old apartments I'd stayed in down there as a college student.

We ended the tour in Los Angeles, and it proved to be a rousing finale. Among the crowd of twenty thousand were many friends, celebrities, and industry types. As usual, Bobby didn't speak during the performance; he just let the songs do the talking for him. Everyone—including me—was quite surprised when, after the last encore, he walked back out to the microphone.

"We want to thank a legendary guy," he said, "who put this whole tour together. Without him, this thing would never have happened."

David Geffen was sitting front and center with Cher, anticipating the sound of his name. Twenty thousand people looked on as he proudly stood up.

"Can you help me give a warm round of applause for Bill Graham!" Bobby shouted.

Geffen practically collapsed back into his seat, stunned. The houselights were on and I could see from my rocking chair how hurt and humiliated he was. He was the one who'd conceived the tour, helped convince Bobby to do it, and brought Graham in. Now Graham was shaking hands with Bobby onstage to the cheers of the crowd, while a mortified Geffen watched sadly from the sidelines.

"Tour '74" had been a huge success and attracted attention around the world. Bobby was on the cover of *Newsweek*, and the demand for tickets was so great that they had to be allocated by lottery. All told, the promoters received some twelve million requests for 650,000 seats—and the reviews were sensational.

Bill Graham had wanted to film the entire tour for posterity, including the concert in San Francisco, his hometown. But Bobby didn't want to. Bill tried as hard as he could to convince Bobby that the footage would be an invaluable asset to him later on. He even agreed to hand over all of the masters at the conclusion of the tour. Bobby wouldn't budge. True to form, he did things his way.

Bill was right, of course. That film should have been made as something to savor for the ages. But then again, perhaps Bobby was ahead of his time on this matter, in feeling as if not every moment should be captured just because, technologically, it could be.

I saw David Geffen backstage after Bobby's slight. His

cheeks were still moist with the tears he had shed. I gave him a hug and went and found Bobby and pulled him aside. I knew he liked David, and appreciated everything he'd done to make the tour happen. When I explained how David had reacted to his little announcement, Bobby was shocked and felt terrible. We agreed to talk in the next few days about how to rectify the situation.

In the scheme of things, Bobby's slight of David was just a little gaffe—but he was determined to make up for it. He visited David's office with Robbie Robertson to personally thank him, and even took out an ad in the *Hollywood Reporter* commending Geffen's many contributions to "Tour '74." I figured that should be enough, but Bobby wasn't through yet. He wanted to do something to honor Geffen, so he asked me to ask Cher what she thought would be a fitting tribute.

When I reached out to her, she told me that David's thirty-first birthday was coming up. How about a nice surprise birthday party? Bobby liked the idea and delegated me to work with Cher to execute it. It was to be a lavish, over-the-top, once-in-a-lifetime affair. Any event of this magnitude needed a theme, but with just two weeks to go, we didn't have one.

What to do?

Bobby decided we needed to have a meeting, and I was mildly curious as to what might transpire. The three of us met at the Regent Beverly Wilshire Hotel, where I was staying. Bobby said he had an idea. He wanted to bring a real carnival to Beverly Hills, complete with knife swallowers, sumo wrestlers, fortune-tellers, mimes, strolling troubadours, sideshows, freak shows—everything and anything we could think of. The event was to be held in the Grand Ballroom of the Regent and Bobby intended to pay for everything.

"No. We split it," said Cher.

And that was that. Now we just had to find a carnival for rent in Beverly Hills.

In the end, the event was nothing short of spectacular. Every star in the firmament was there, including some from other galaxies. Cher and Bobby led everyone in singing "Happy Birthday" to David; then Cher and Rick Danko sang "Mockingbird," and Bobby and Cher sang "All I Really Want to Do," accompanied by The Band. In one of the highlights of the evening, a four-hundred-pound sumo wrestler came hurtling by at ninety miles an hour and nearly took out Robbie Robertson.

Bobby brought the show to a fitting ending by singing "Mr. Tambourine Man" for David. As David and Cher were leaving, I noticed he had a big smile on his face. (Well, who wouldn't, when exiting with Cher?) Mission accomplished. I guess we should all hope to be slighted by Bob Dylan!

Perhaps the surprise party was a harbinger, because something about the music and the carnival atmosphere seemed to linger in Bobby's consciousness for days afterward. Soon he would attempt something very different from anything he or anybody else in the music business had ever tried before.

EIGHT

Will the Real Idiot Please Stand Up?

Coming off "Tour '74," Bobby's creative juices were flowing big time. When I came back from Alaska in July, I went to see Bobby at his place outside Minneapolis, and he played me the songs he had written. These would constitute his critically acclaimed album *Blood on the Tracks*, and I was one of the first people to hear them.

"Crosby, Stills, Nash & Young are playing tonight in Saint Paul," he said. "Do you want to go with me?"

We went to the concert, which was at the Saint Paul Civic Center. Afterward, we went to the hotel where the band was staying. Bill Graham and Barry Imhoff were the tour promoters, so we had a chance to see and visit with them again. After a while, Bobby mentioned to Stephen Stills that he had just written some new songs and of course Stephen wanted to hear them. So Bobby, Stephen, and I went into the bedroom of the suite and Bobby played a few things.

Stephen was obviously loaded, and when Bobby sang "Idiot Wind," he became paranoid and very agitated.

"You wrote that song about me!" he shouted. "Why did you write that song about me?"

He jumped up and got right in Bobby's face. As Bobby's friend and self-appointed protector, I jumped in between them so Stephen couldn't get any closer. Carefully, I eased Stephen back.

Bobby just laughed and said, "Relax, man; the song's not about you," as he continued to sing and strum without missing a beat.

Millions of people around the world identify personally with Bobby's songs and feel as if he is speaking directly to them. But few of them are loaded enough to think the songs were actually written about them.

In early December 1974, Bobby and I were in New York together when I had a meeting with a big player in the fish business. His name was Aaron and he had the largest smoked fish and pickled herring operation in the country. Bobby wanted to come to the meeting, so I introduced him as my friend Robert. He just sat there quietly while we took care of business, taking it all in.

Afterward, he said, "That guy was really sharp. It would be worth it to pay him to just follow me around and look after my interests."

When I saw Aaron again at a national seafood convention six months later and told him what Bobby had said, he admitted that he'd had no idea who "Robert" was. But after we'd left, all the young people in his office had freaked out. As he told it, "They came running up to me shouting, 'Do you know who that was?'"

"Yeah ... that was Louie Kemp," I said, having no clue what the shouting was about.

"'No! The other guy!'" one of them said. "'That was Bob Dylan!'"

A few days later, Bobby and I flew up to Toronto to catch his friend George Harrison's concert with Ravi Shankar. This was the first tour by a Beatle since their breakup. Bobby and George got to spend a little quality time together after the show.

In late December, Bobby went back to work on *Blood on the Tracks*, rerecording five of the songs in a Minneapolis studio. The album was released in January of 1975, and it immediately rocketed to number one on Billboard's Hot 100 chart. Since then, it has become one of Bobby's most widely admired and best-selling albums.

NINE

The Godfather, and Bobby Too

I got to know Marlon Brando through a mutual friend, and his son, Christian, came to work for me at my fisheries in Alaska and Duluth. Although many notorious stories have been told about him over the years, Marlon impressed me as a dedicated parent. He would often call me to check up on his boy, exhibiting all of the tenacious and loving concern of a Jewish mother. *Was he eating enough? Did he get to work on time? Was he hanging out with the right people?* Christian was a great kid. He worked hard, had a good attitude, and earned the respect of all his coworkers.

Bill Graham knew I was friends with Marlon, so one day, a few months after *Blood on the Tracks* was released, he called me.

"I'm going to do this huge benefit concert," he said, "to buy athletic equipment for the San Francisco public school system. They have budget problems, and it's my community, so I'm going to help them raise money for the kids."

"That's great, Bill," I said. "How can I help you?"

"Well ..." he continued, "I think the crowd would love it if Marlon Brando would come as a surprise guest and speak. Do you think you could ask him if he'd be up for that?"

I called Marlon and made the request.

After listening to the details, he said, "Tell Bill, if he'll give a donation to the American Indians from the proceeds, I'll do it. As long as you go with me."

Bill agreed to Marlon's terms, and so did I.

The benefit featured a wide variety of musicians, celebrities, and athletes in addition to Bobby and Marlon. The Grateful Dead was there, as was Jefferson Airplane, the Doobie Brothers, baseball legend Willie Mays, and hometown favorites Carlos Santana and Joan Baez. The event was held at Kezar Stadium, which supposedly had a capacity crowd of almost sixty thousand.

Just after Jefferson Airplane performed, Bill Graham took the stage and surprised the crowd by introducing Marlon. He was greeted with thunder from the crowd, and gave a heartfelt address about helping all the poor people of all nationalities.

"I'm going to give five thousand bucks to the show," he said. "We gotta give, give, and give. We gotta give of our feelings. If we haven't got anything but our feelings, let's give that. Because that counts more than every fucking piece of money in the world. If you got a penny, a nickel. If you got an old hat that you don't need—make a contribution of something."

The crowd roared as Marlon came off the stage, seemingly dazed. Gesturing to the crowd, he said to Graham, "And they weren't extras!"

Toward the end of the concert, Graham came back on yet again.

"And now, to close it out," he said, "may I introduce on bass, Rick Danko; on keyboards, Garth Hudson; on drums, Levon Helm; on guitar, Tim Drummond; on pedal steel, Ben Keith; on guitar and piano, Neil Young; and on harmonica and guitar … Bob Dylan!"

The crowd went crazy. Bobby, his hair long, curly, and wild, performed a few rousing numbers, closing with "Knockin' on Heaven's Door." For the encore, he sang the old Carter Family hymn, "Can the Circle Be Unbroken."

After nine hours, the show was finally over except the endless ovations (and, presumably, donations).

After the concert, Marlon invited me to dinner at the house of a friend of his. We pulled up to an imposing Victorian mansion, and when the door opened, out came Francis Ford Coppola—who had directed Marlon in *The Godfather*. (They hadn't yet embarked on the adventure that was to become *Apocalypse Now*.) Warm greetings and introductions were exchanged, and we proceeded inside.

The atmosphere and decor felt very traditionally Italian. Francis's wife and daughters were busy preparing a fabulous meal, and when it was served, Francis sat at the head of the table with Marlon to his right.

On the flight back to Los Angeles, Marlon told me he was happy he had come. He'd been extraordinarily moved by the energy and excitement of the crowd of sixty thousand young people.

"It was contagious," he said. "I usually perform on a movie set, and there is no feedback from a live audience.

The energy coming back at you from a large crowd is so exciting! These rock-and-roll people, they get to play off live crowds. I really envy them that."

Later that night, after we'd gone our separate ways, Marlon was on my mind. I thought about how fortunate I was to have met and hung out with someone who'd been an inspiration to me. He'd inspired James Dean and Bob Dylan too. I had to wonder, who *didn't* Marlon Brando inspire? Yet, I'd seen him be inspired by a crowd of cheering kids.

TEN

Summer of '75

I'd been busy in Alaska running my seafood company, shipping millions of pounds of salmon, mostly to Japan. Now back in Duluth, I was just unpacking my suitcase when the phone rang. It was Bobby. He invited me to come down to his farm, about forty miles north of Minneapolis. And, could I stay for a while? He had some ideas he wanted to run by me.

So I repacked my suitcase and hit the road.

When Bobby decided he "wasn't gonna work on Maggie's farm no more," he did what every good Jewish businessman does: he bought his own. The area around his place seemed straight out of the 1950s and still going strong. A lone hardware store, a weather-beaten drive-in restaurant, and a Red Owl grocery store lined the single paved street that constituted the "town." I finally found the right earth-and-gravel road that led to Bobby's place, which was unmarked except for a black mailbox. I pulled up to a one-story farmhouse that anybody would have called nondescript except for the fact that Bob Dylan was standing on the porch smiling at me like he'd just eaten the canary in the coal mine.

Bobby was clearly excited, and not for the first time, I wondered what the hell he was up to. After exchanging just a few words about the drive, he led me to one of the kids' rooms, where I stashed my stuff, and then back down to the kitchen, where iced tea was waiting. There was no air-conditioning in the place though the weather was hotter than nine kinds of hell. Instead, ceiling fans were swirling madly in high gear, and so was Bobby.

As we sipped and talked, he told me that he'd been taking art lessons from painter Norman Raeben, son of the famed writer Sholem Aleichem. He raved about the classes, said they gave him a deeper understanding of creativity, a fresh take on songwriting. Then he said he had some new music to share. He proceeded to play some cuts off his not-yet-released album, *Desire*. The moment I heard the songs, I knew they were important, and that they would have a deep impact on fans and musicians alike for years to come. I told Bobby as much.

Inscrutable as ever, he just kept smiling.

We spent the next few days talking about old times: the things we had dreamed of as kids, the fancy cherry-red cars we'd said we'd buy when we got rich, along with the fur coats we'd get for our mothers. By this point, we'd both bought a few of each.

Some afternoons, we'd wander out back to the Crow River, which flowed through the property, and take a little rowboat out for a spin. In the evenings, we'd play basketball. Bobby was a good player with a tricky pivot shot that was always accompanied by raucous laughter as he made the basket. He played basketball like he made music, endlessly surprising and amusing to those fortunate enough to be present to witness the display. With Bobby, life itself was a pivot shot.

The days ticked by, but Bobby continued to keep his new plans close to the vest. This was typical; he'd come out with what he wanted to say when he was ready, and not before.

One particularly hot afternoon, after a long game of one-on-one, we'd just sat down for our iced-tea ritual and, as Bobby poured, he told me he had an idea for a tour. He wanted it to be much different from "Tour '74." He was not interested in doing another tour of giant venues, or going from city to city in a private jet—and I could empathize, having been along on that wild ride. Instead, he wanted to play theaters, small clubs, colleges, and unusual venues; and, instead of a high-powered entourage, he wanted to assemble a kind of gypsy caravan of performers traveling in a circus-like atmosphere. He wasn't looking to make money, he said—just to have fun. This would be a tour that the fans and performers could enjoy equally.

Bobby told me that he had already pitched the idea to the big New York promoters, as well as to people at his label, Columbia Records. All of them had nixed the idea.

"Take advantage of your talent and fame," they'd told him. "Do a big tour; sell out as many huge halls and stadiums as you can." In other words, *make a lot of money*.

They just didn't get what he was trying to do. And, had I not been with Bobby throughout "Tour '74," I might not have gotten it either. This "gypsy caravan" idea may have been a bit crazy and farfetched, but it immediately appealed to me as much as it did to Bobby. It was righteous, different, and real, just like him. Just like his music.

When I thought about it, it wasn't the least bit surprising that Bobby was in danger of getting trapped by his own success—or that he knew it. This plan was his way of avoiding the jaws of that trap.

"What do you think of the idea?" he asked when he finally stopped talking and took a sip of tea.

"Screw 'em if they can't take a joke," I said.

"We won't even announce where the band will play," he said. "We won't even tell the other musicians. It'll be a mystery for them too. We'll swoop into town and before they know it, we'll be gone—like the Lone Ranger!" Bobby smiled, pleased with his own ingenuity. Then he smiled even wider. "Louie ... will you produce the tour for me?"

Not too many things Bobby said surprised me at that point, but this did. "Produce the tour? I've never produced anything in my life, other than fish!"

Bobby shrugged.

"Louis," he said calmly, "you can sell fish; you can sell tickets."

It was an unbelievable offer. My childhood friend—now a rock icon—wanted me to produce a full-scale tour. I knew he was serious. I also knew that his judgment tended to be impeccable and his decision-making process methodical. I thought back over the months I'd spent in that rocking chair on stage next to Levon Helm. Now I wondered if all that had been on-the-job training. Could it be that he'd wanted me to absorb the nuts and bolts of the music business without any pressure? Was it possible that he'd known all along that he might make me this offer one day?

"You're a successful businessman," he said, by way of reassuring me. "And you can't deny that you've seen it all from the inside. If anybody can put this thing together, it's you."

Bobby's enthusiasm was infectious, and I certainly didn't want to disappoint him the way the New York promoters and his label had. Besides, I shared his vision. I could almost see his great rock-and-roll carnival taking shape in the moist air of his country kitchen.

I had only a vague idea of the magnitude of what I was getting myself into, but I thought about it for just thirty seconds before saying, "OK, let's do it."

He beamed me his best, most mischievous and mystical smile.

"I'll put together the band and the show," he said. "You take care of everything else."

I nodded, not exactly knowing what "everything else" was, but knowing I'd figure it out somehow. For Bobby and for the challenge of it.

"Deal," I said.

As we shook hands, I couldn't tell if it was my head spinning or the ceiling fan above us. It was mid-July and Bobby wanted to launch the tour in late October—just a few months away. I had my work cut out for me.

Later, Bobby walked me to my car, still smiling encouragingly.

"My people will call your people," I joked.

The problem was, in the business of music, I didn't have any people.

ELEVEN

Birth of the "Rolling Thunder Revue"

On the way back to Duluth, I got to thinking. I had just over three months to get this whole thing together. I'd promised I'd get back to him with all the details, but one thing in particular was already beginning to bother me. How could anybody—let alone a novice—launch a viable national tour without mentioning the two words that were the key to its success: *Bob Dylan*? But that's what Bobby had specified, so that's what I would have to do.

Observing Bill Graham in action had been like a master class in the business of rock-tour execution. And, as luck would have it, I learned that his former business partner, Barry Imhoff, had left Graham to go solo just weeks before. I knew I didn't have a prayer of getting Graham to work for me as tour director, but Barry would be the next best thing.

As soon as I got back to Duluth, I called Barry, to whom I'd become pretty close during "Tour '74." I told him we were going to attempt something that no major rock act had ever done before, and I described the autonomous, grassroots caravan that Bobby had envisioned, featuring loads of other big-name performers in a carnival atmosphere.

"It's meant to be a kind of traveling minstrel show," I explained. "We're not going to use conventional publicists or concert promoters or anything; we'll do it all ourselves. We'll announce concert dates just two or three days in advance in each market, and sell tickets first come, first serve." I paused, and when he didn't jump in, I said, "And one more thing, Barry. We're not going to bill it as a Bob Dylan concert. It'll be a kind of *musical experience,* featuring a revolving roster of musicians, performers, and actors of every stripe."

What was Barry going to say to all this? I couldn't wait to hear the reaction of the first person from inside the music industry who might be crazy enough to share our vision and help make it happen. I knew he was a no-bullshit straight shooter, so I was a bit nervous as I held the phone and waited for his reply.

"Fascinating," he said. "I love it. No one has ever attempted anything like this, let alone a superstar like Bob."

Barry was in! Not just in, but passionate about the idea, and committed to making it a success. With his contacts, he said, he could provide the very best technical and support people. *Hey, maybe we can pull this off!* I thought.

I told Barry that if I hired him, I'd have to have the final say on everything, including who got hired, where we'd play, how much money we'd spend on what, how and where the shows got publicized—everything. Barry agreed to my terms and I hired him on the spot. I explained that we wanted to start the tour in New England.

I was about to hang up when Barry stopped me.

"But wait, Louie," he said. "What are we going to call this thing?"

That was a good question and I didn't have an answer. I told him I'd get back to him with the name and more details. Then I hung up and called Bobby at the farm, eager to tell him that things were already in motion.

After I'd filled him in, I said, "By the way ... what do you want to call the tour?"

He hummed to himself for a moment or two, then said, "Let's call it the 'Rolling Thunder Revue.'"

Things began to move rapidly. Barry brought two "Tour '74" veterans, Gary Shafner and Michael Ahern, aboard. Their job was to map out the tour schedule and fill it in with potential venues. Barry would then send me the various options for comment and selection. I told him I wanted to kick off around Halloween, in a Plymouth, Massachusetts, auditorium. Somehow, the evocation of pilgrims and goblins seemed fitting for the first page of our musical adventure.

Per my instructions, Barry didn't even tell Gary and Michael who the principle attraction was; they had no idea that they were planning a tour for Bob Dylan, and neither did anyone else. Bobby remained serious about breaking all the rules, and creating something creative rather than star driven, and I respected that to the letter.

I flew to San Francisco and then drove to Sausalito to visit the ground operation, which was set up in the living room of Barry's house. The place looked like a war room whose occupants had a penchant for pepperoni pizza. There was a big map of New England and eastern Canada on the wall, with different-colored pins stuck into various locations. There were half-eaten sandwiches and empty soda bottles strewn around on tables and chairs, and through the big oval window in Barry's living room, you could see the San Francisco Bay, complete with seagulls and the little boats rising and falling in front of the Golden Gate Bridge. It seemed a conducive spot for planning a musical mystery tour.

From there, I flew to the City of Angels and made a base camp at the Chateau Marmont on the Sunset Strip. When I thought I had everything lined up, I drove out to Malibu to present the whole tour plan to Bobby and get his final approval. As I drove north on the Pacific Coast Highway, even the tanned girls playing beach volleyball in their bikinis couldn't distract me from my mission.

Bobby ushered me in and we got right down to it. As I enthusiastically began to lay out all the plans and specifics of what had up until that point been just a dream to Bobby, he seemed genuinely surprised.

It was exactly the reaction I'd expected. It's always a surprise to see a vision become a reality. I knew his heart was in it; I just had to be sure that his mind was as well. After all, the core personnel were in place now, the itinerary was all but finalized, and we'd even put a hold on some of the venues.

On several occasions, Bobby had told me, "the country-and-western guys got it right." He liked the way they performed a hundred-plus shows a year, traveling in elaborate, comfortable tour buses that were like homes on wheels. "That's the way to tour," he'd told me. "Those guys are the real musicians because they're always on the road performing and they truly live for their music."

With that in mind, I showed him a picture of a particularly sharp-looking tour bus that had often been used on country-and-western tours.

He loved it. Which was good, because I'd already lined it up for him.

Finally, I got around to asking him if he'd decided who he wanted to come play with him. Had he talked to anyone yet? He said he still had to do that, and I reminded him that we were opening in eight weeks in Plymouth. The truth is, Bobby was a bit taken aback that I'd put so much together—right down to the most minute details—in such a brief period, while he had still not taken care of his part of our deal.

"Everything sounds great," he said. "Let me think about it."

Now it was my turn to be taken aback. I told him I was leaving town in two days and I had to have a confirmation that the thing was a go before I left, or I would have to cancel everything.

"I'll be leaving my room at the Chateau Marmont at five o'clock on Tuesday," I said, "and going straight to the airport. If I don't hear from you before then, I'm going to close it down."

By late Tuesday afternoon, I still hadn't heard from

Bobby. My bags were packed and I was pacing back and forth in my room at the Chateau. I had my hand on the doorknob ready to go and check out when the phone finally rang. It was precisely 4:59. It was Bobby.

"Louie," he said, "let's do it."

If he'd waited just a minute or two longer, one of the greatest tours of all time might never have happened. He knew what was at stake as well as I did, but in typical Bobby style, he'd remained mysterious right up to the last possible moment.

TWELVE

You'll Never Work in Rock and Roll Again

We decided to do the pre-tour preparations and rehearsals in New York City. We booked rooms at the Gramercy Park Hotel, and, through a friend, Barry found us some unused office space in Midtown.

Bobby had done his job and put together a fantastic band that included Rob Stoner, Howie Wyeth, T Bone Burnett, Mick Ronson, Steven Soles, and Scarlet Rivera. He also recruited Joan Baez, Roger McGuinn, Ramblin' Jack Elliott, and Bob Neuwirth to perform, and Jacques Levy to orchestrate. The plan was, while we were in New York, those of us working on the logistical aspects of the tour would go to work every day in the office. Meanwhile, Bobby and the other artists would rehearse and develop the show.

Bobby had decided he wanted to shoot a movie during the tour, and asked me to find Howard Alk, a filmmaker he'd worked with in the past. I tracked him down in Canada, and when I told him about the project, he was excited to come on board.

As the film crew was coming together, Bobby said, "There's this hip playwright named Sam Shepard. I like his work. Get a hold of him and see if he'll join us to write a script for the movie."

So I tracked Sam down in San Francisco, got him on the phone, and told him all about it.

"Is this for real?" he asked. "And who are you?"

Once I'd managed to convince him that I actually worked with Bobby and the whole thing was on the level, he was intrigued. Sam was a fan of Bobby's, and the possibility of working with him on something out of the mainstream won him over.

"Great," I said. "I'll arrange a plane ticket for you. Can you get here in two days?"

"I can be there," he said, "but I don't fly. Just don't like it. How about if I take the train?"

When it became clear that I wasn't going to change his mind about flying, I arranged a train ticket for him and told Bobby the good news.

As long as we're waiting for Sam to cross the country by train, here's a little side note about him—something that happened years after "Rolling Thunder" was history.

In 1987, I got a call from Sam, saying he was in Duluth.

"What the hell are you doing in Duluth?" I asked.

He said he was preparing to shoot a movie called *Far North*, and was scouting locations and looking for a place to live while filming. I asked him about the time frame, and I guess God was smiling on us, because it turned out I was not going to be in Duluth when he was shooting. So

I gave Sam my address and told him to come over, that I might have just the place for him.

At the time, I had the good fortune to be the owner/caretaker of an 8,000-square-foot mansion on five acres, right on the shore of Lake Superior. The Congdons, the wealthiest family in Duluth, had developed the property, having made their fortune in iron-ore mines near Hibbing, where Bobby grew up.

I was happy to see Sam again, and we reminisced about our experiences on "Rolling Thunder." He told me that Jessica Lange would be starring in *Far North* and that she was from Cloquet, a small town twenty miles away. He was looking for accommodations for Jessica and himself and their young daughter, Hannah.

He loved the house and property, and was very pleased when I told him he was free to live there during the shoot. There was only one condition, I said. I kept a kosher kitchen, and he would have to replace the sinks when he left. I explained that you can't re-kosher porcelain since it is porous. Sam readily agreed, and—true to his word—he arranged to have the new fixtures installed when he moved out.

Back at "Rolling Thunder" headquarters, Bobby decided we needed a car to get around New York City—preferably a Cadillac convertible. I called Naomi, who was in charge of all of Bobby's business affairs, and asked her if she could get me some cash. Then Barry and I went car shopping. The Cadillac dealership in Manhattan had a sweet red

Caddie Eldorado convertible on hand. We negotiated for a while, then I pulled out a wad of hundreds and peeled them off. Before the sales guy could stop scratching his head in amazement, we drove off in it.

A few days later, Bobby took the car out on the town, and the next morning, he reported that it had been towed ... with one of his guitars in the trunk. Gary Shafner and I found the impound location and rushed over there. Once we'd paid the fees, we opened the trunk, and, to our great relief, there it was: the beautiful, classic 1963 Martin acoustic D-28. That guitar would soon be worth more than the car. In fact, in November 2017, it sold at auction for $396,000!

A whole group of us went out each night, often to someplace in the Village. Wherever we went, Bobby would bump into a friend or two and end up inviting new people—like Ronee Blakley and Allen Ginsberg—to join the show and entourage.

When I talked to violinist Scarlet Rivera about those days, she recalled, "I was walking on 13th Street, in the East Village, with my violin case over my shoulder, when a nondescript green car pulled up alongside me. Bob rolled down the window and asked, 'Can you play that thing?' and I answered, 'I sure can.' Suddenly the topic was gypsy music, which was very intuitive, as he hadn't heard me play yet. He was insistent that he hear me play, and I agreed to get in the car. Soon we were at his loft, and he told me just to play along with whatever I heard. He chose to play only unreleased songs with no hint of what key or a chart—not wanting to make it easy for me. We played song after song, with no comment whatsoever. Then he moved to an upright piano and again, I played along. Still no comment. Finally, he closed the piano lid, and, with a little smile, said he wanted to go see a friend of his perform nearby, and did I want to come along?

"Soon we were at the Bottom Line to see Muddy Waters and his band. At one point during the set, while I sat at the bar, Bob went up onstage. I guess you can imagine what a big reception there was when people saw that Bob Dylan was there! Anyway, he played a song, and at the end of it, he went to the mic and announced, 'Now, I want to bring up my violinist!' I was pretty shocked—but I grabbed my violin, scrambled from the bar to the stage as the song started, and began playing along. Pretty soon, Muddy threw me a solo, and all eyes of the band and the audience were on me. I saw Muddy and Bob scrutinizing my playing … and halfway through my solo, they smiled.

"After the show, the entire band piled into a couple of cars and headed to Brooklyn to visit the blues legend Victoria Spivey, and we all talked and sang and played together till dawn. Bob drove me home and asked for my number. Two days later, he called me and told me to come to CBS Studios the next morning.

"That was the beginning of recording his album *Desire*. When I got there, I found Eric Clapton and his band, along with a bunch of the top New York session players.

I created my own parts and barely talked to anyone. Bob listened carefully to all of the tracks at the end of the day, and told me, 'Come back tomorrow.' I think, besides evaluating every note and phrase I played, he was scanning my character. If he hadn't liked *that*, I would not have ended up on *Desire*, and I certainly wouldn't have been the first woman band member of the 'Rolling Thunder Revue.'"

As the entourage grew, so did the movie crew and our expenses. But I had a plan. As I explained to Bobby, his records were already selling up a storm, his fan base was enormous, and his new album, *Desire*, would just make it bigger. There was no question the tour would generate a lot of interest, and that would translate into a lot of money for Columbia Records. I wanted to ask Columbia to provide some financial support for the tour.

"I don't know if they'll do that," he said, "but it would be nice if you could get them to help out."

"I'm going straight to the president of the label," I said. My mother always told me that when you want to get something done, go to the head, not the tail.

I called Naomi and told her my plan, and she was pretty pessimistic. She said she had tried to get promotional money from them in the past, and they'd always said no.

"Never hurts to try again," I said. Then I asked her who the president of Columbia Records was, and how to reach him by phone. She gave me the information, but laughed at me, saying I was wasting my time.

My first call got me as far as the assistant for Walter Yetnikoff, the president of the largest record company in the world.

"I'm Louie Kemp," I said to her, "and I represent Bob Dylan. I'm the producer of a new tour he's going to do, and I want to meet with Mr. Yetnikoff so we can coordinate with Columbia to maximize the benefit of the tour for everybody."

She asked for my number, and said she would speak to Mr. Yetnikoff and get back to me. In very short order, she called me back and said her boss would be happy to meet with me. When did I want to come over?

Why wait? The next day, I went over to Columbia Records. It was headquartered in the CBS building on the corner of West 52nd and Sixth Avenue, an imposing building dubbed "Black Rock" for its dark granite cladding. I was ushered into Mr. Yetnikoff's office, which was enormous, with a great view. The walls were decorated with pictures of stars and gold records.

Walter was friendly and warm.

"I'm so happy Bob is going out on tour," he said. "It'll be great for his record sales. And I'm happy you came to see me, so we can coordinate our efforts. We want to be sure that the record stores in the tour cities are well stocked, and we want to give store people and radio DJs tickets to the concerts, for publicity purposes. You know, Columbia is proud to have Bob on the roster; we're so happy he's in such a productive stage of his career."

Before I could get a word in, Yetnikoff barreled on.

"'Tour '74' was amazing. His *Blood on the Tracks* album was brilliant. And I understand from Don DeVito that he has another album coming. If you give us the itinerary, I'll get back to you with our ticket needs for each concert."

Let me just pause for a second here to clarify that in those days, before the Internet and social media and all, record companies relied heavily on radio DJs and record store owners to promote shows. In order to get them talking, they handed out lots of complimentary tickets.

"Well, Walter," I said when he came up for air, "this tour is going to be a lot different from any previous ones. In fact, we think it's going to make history. You see, the shows will be in small venues and the lineup will be kind of free-form. We're only going to announce the shows and sell tickets a few days before they happen. In fact, even the performers on the tour won't know where the shows are going to be. We're going to break all the rules, make the shows all about the music and the audience, not the promoters and the label. And, by the way, we'll be shooting a movie of the whole thing."

Walter's eyes had been getting wider and wider as I talked, and when I finished he couldn't suppress a huge smile.

Before he could frame a response, I added, "Anyway, Walter, maybe you're wondering why I'm here. It's not just to 'coordinate.' We're going to need $100,000 from Columbia to help support tour expenses."

His smile vanished.

"We don't do that," he said. "If we did that for Bob, we would have to do that for everyone, and—"

"Well that's too bad," I cut in. "Because if I can't count on Columbia to be a good, supportive partner for Bob and the tour, then we aren't going to be able to supply you with the itinerary or any tickets."

"But," he exploded, "we *have* to have tickets! We *have* to know where Bob is going to be playing. We're his label. We'd be humiliated if we weren't a part of this!"

Maybe it seems crazy, considering to whom I was talking and where I was standing, but I was feeling pretty bold.

"Walter," I said quietly, "if you don't show Bob your good faith by putting some of your cash in the pot, then you can find out about the tour in the paper or on the radio, just like everybody else. Who knows? If you work at it, you can probably score some tickets on the street."

With that, I turned and acted like I was about to walk out of his office, secretly hoping he'd stop me—which is exactly what he did.

"OK, OK!" he yelled. "We'll contribute $100,000. But we need access."

Yes.

"All right, Walter," I said, still dead calm. "Please have the check delivered to Bob's office tomorrow. I'll leave the address with your assistant."

"It'll be there."

Negotiating with Walter wasn't really that different from dealing with the Japanese, to whom I sold most of my Alaskan fish. If you had what they wanted, they would eventually pay your price.

When I told Naomi to expect the check, she was in shock.

"The whole $100,000? How'd you get him to pay that?"

"I just smothered him with love and kindness," I replied.

Of course, Bobby was happy, too.

"Good job, Louie," he said, then went back to his job, which was being Bob Dylan.

A couple of days later, Bobby and the film crew were brainstorming different possibilities for behind-the-scenes footage, since we wanted to have elements of "the making of the tour" as part of the storyline. I suggested that we go over to CBS, where I could introduce Bobby to Walter, because—believe it or not—they'd never met. I also suggested we make it a surprise visit.

"Let's do it," said Bobby.

So we headed over to Black Rock with the film crew in tow. When we entered the big lobby with the cameras rolling, security immediately came running over.

"Hey! No cameras allowed in here," said the smaller of the two guards. "What do you think you're doing?"

"We're here to see Mr. Yetnikoff," I said politely.

"Do you have an appointment?"

"No, we don't."

"You and your whole crew—you've gotta leave right

now," said the bigger guy, who was now standing practically on my toes.

"We're not going anywhere," I said. "I suggest you call Mr. Yetnikoff and let him know that Bob Dylan and Louie Kemp are here to see him."

At the sound of Bobby's name, he glanced around, then held my gaze for few seconds.

"Fine," he said. "Just stay right where you are. Don't move."

He went over to the desk, made a call, and, after a few moments, came back to us.

"I'll escort you upstairs," he said, as we followed him to the elevators, "but you can't film. Turn off your cameras."

We made a show of doing as he said, but obviously, we had no intention of really shutting off the equipment. We were there to get some footage, and we were getting good stuff!

As we exited the elevator, Walter's assistant was waiting for us.

"Welcome back, Mr. Kemp," she said. "Walter is waiting for you."

As we turned the corner toward his office, I could see that the door was open and he was standing in the middle of the room.

"Walter," I said, "this is Bob. I thought it was time that you two met."

"I'm pleased that you came over, Bob," said Walter, barely glancing at the camera crew. "I have always been a big admirer of your work, and on behalf of Columbia Records,

I want you to know that we're honored that you're with us. Louie has told me about your upcoming tour. It sounds fantastic."

"Walter, I want to thank you for your cash support," said Bobby.

"Well, I want you to know that we consider ourselves your partner in whatever you want to do. You can always count on us. Why don't you sit down and get comfortable?"

Ignoring the invitation, Bobby roamed around the large office, looking out the windows and at all of the memorabilia lining the walls. The cameras rolled relentlessly on, until, at long last, Bobby spoke.

"You've got a nice view here, Walter. If I had this view, I'd never get anything done."

"Yes," said Walter, "I guess it can be distracting."

By the third time Walter asked if he wanted any coffee, Bobby was gone. Like the Lone Ranger, he'd accomplished his mission and vanished, leaving the rest of us mortals to ask, "Who was that masked man?"

Whoever he was and wherever he went, he rejoined us at the elevator. I still remember all of us laughing uncontrollably on the way down.

Some years later, my sister, Sharon, was at Dan Tana's restaurant in L.A. when she was introduced to a couple of friends of friends, including Walter Yetnikoff. When Walter heard her last name, he said, "You're not related to Louie Kemp are you?"

"Yes," replied Sharon innocently, "he's my brother. Do you know him?"

"DO I KNOW YOUR BROTHER?" Walter shouted, jumping up from the table. "Let me tell you what *your brother* did to me. He ambushed me twice! The first time, he shook me down for $100,000 of the company's money. Then, a few days later, I'm sitting in my office and a security guard calls me from the lobby to tell me there's a whole camera crew down there, and a couple of weird guys insisting that they want to see me. 'Should we throw them out?' he asks. 'One of them is supposed to be Bob Dylan and the other one is named Louie Kemp. They're dressed like hippies.'

"Now, I had waited years to meet Bob Dylan," he went on, "and this dumb guard was about to throw him out of the building!" He sat back down and leaned in toward my sister, whose mouth had dropped open. "I'll never forget that name: *Louie Kemp!*"

We needed an advance person to take charge of ticketing and get the word out to the public about each show. Barry suggested a guy named Jerry Seltzer from San Francisco, who had been in charge of ticketing for the Roller Derby for years. He knew the guy, and proceeded to recruit him for us.

Here's how Jerry remembers it: "One day, I got a call from Barry about some super-secret music tour. Since I was the best ticket man he knew—and probably the only one—he wanted me to come to New York to help set things up.

"When I got to New York and met with Barry, he swore me to secrecy and told me about Bob and Joan Baez, and the other people who were going to be touring. There wasn't going to be any computerized ticketing, no artists listed on the tickets, and no pre-publicity.

When I agreed to work on the thing, I was given a mobile home, two assistants, and told to go to each city a few days ahead of time and pass out handbills announcing the tour. Handbills! Even in the seventies, this was a crazy way of promoting a tour! But I did as I was told, and, you know what? It worked out."

Jerry might have thought we were crazy, but neither Bobby nor I was worried. In the end, every show was sold out, and we never spent a penny on publicity!

The planning, rehearsing, and partying phase in New York lasted three weeks, and then it was time to get moving for our first gig, which was scheduled for the Plymouth Memorial Hall on October 30—the night before Hallow-een—just as we'd envisioned. The company was booked to stay at the Sea Crest Beach Hotel in North Falmouth, about thirty-five miles away, and we'd rented a house nearby for Bobby.

The night before we were to leave New York, we were all hanging out in the bar at the Gramercy Park Hotel. I stayed until about midnight, then told Bobby I was going up to my room to try to get a good night's sleep. I reminded him that we had a big travel day coming up, and suggested he do the same.

"Don't worry, Louie. I will," he said.

I told Gary, whom I'd tasked with looking out for Bobby when I wasn't around, to try to get him to wrap it up as soon as possible. Gary was a special guy—smart, trustworthy, a hard worker, and loyal, and he had a very dry sense of humor. It's no wonder he ended up being Bobby's road manager for fifteen years. As I got in the elevator, I felt confident that Bobby was in good hands.

I crawled into my bed, happy that I'd get a good night's sleep, not knowing when I'd get another one. On the road, we tended to stay up pretty late.

So there I was, fast asleep in Louie World, when my serenity was breached by the sound of pounding on the door and a voice screaming, "Louie! Louie! Get up! GET UP!"

My eyes snapped open.

Nope. Not a dream.

I staggered to the door, threw it open, and found a panicky Raven, a.k.a. Jeff Bloom.

"Louie," he shouted, "you have to come right now! Gary sent me to get you. Bob is trying to leave and drive alone to Falmouth."

"Gimme a minute and don't let him go anywhere," I mumbled, and closed the door in the poor guy's face.

I grabbed my pants and a shirt, and got dressed as I lurched toward the elevator. Halfway down to the lobby, I realized I wasn't wearing shoes. *Too late now.* I raced out to the street and spotted the camper near the front entrance of the hotel. Bobby was behind the wheel and Gary was holding the door open in spite of Bobby's repeated orders to "Close the damn door so I can get the hell out of here!"

"Hi, you guys," I said cheerily, as if I'd run into them at a swap meet. "What's going on?"

"Bob wants to leave now for Falmouth," said Gary. "And he wants to drive."

"Bob," I said, "don't you want to wait for everybody else, and leave at 10:00 a.m. like we planned?"

"No," said Bobby. "I'm ready and I want to go NOW."

"Well … OK," I replied, keeping it totally cool. "That's not a problem, if that's what you want. But you've had a few drinks, so I think maybe Gary should drive you. Being sober and all."

"No, Louie, I'm fine. I don't need Gary or anybody else to drive me."

"The thing is … it's my responsibility to make that decision," I said. "And I just can't let you drive. So, why don't you move over to the passenger seat, sit back, and enjoy the ride to New England."

"You can't tell me what to do, Louie!" said Bob. "Now, get out of my way, or I'll see that you never work in rock-and-roll again!"

"Look, Bobby, I don't give a shit about working in rock-and-roll. I have the fish business. It's doing pretty good, and fish don't talk back; you know what I mean? I'm only doing this because we're friends. We *are* friends, right, Bobby? And a friend would never let a friend drink and drive, so …"

Bobby could see that he wasn't going to get a rise out of me, and he certainly wasn't going to get me to back off.

"OK, OK, Looooouie," he whined. "If you insist, Gary can drive."

"Good. I'm glad that's all settled," I said. "Now, shove the hell over so Gary can get in. And Gary, if you let Bob drive, I'll kill you."

"OK, Looooouie," Gary whined in imitation of Bob.

When they were both tucked in and ready to roll, I wished them a nice ride and told them I'd see them in the afternoon. I slammed the camper door shut and watched with relief as it headed off slowly and turned the corner.

I went back to bed feeling pretty good about my skills of persuasion. What I didn't know was that as soon as they'd rounded the bend, Bobby had ordered Gary to pull over.

Throwing the passenger door open, he shouted, "Get out! I'm going to drive myself."

"Bob, please," Gary pleaded. "Louie will kill me. At least … don't throw me out. Let me ride along with you."

Being a big-hearted kind of guy, Bobby reluctantly said, "OK. You take shotgun."

With Gary keeping an eagle eye on him, Bobby drove through the night, straight to the nice house on the water that Barry had rented for him.

"OK, Bobby, we made it," Gary said. "Let's check the place out."

"You go on," Bobby mumbled. "I'll be there in a minute or two."

When I arrived that afternoon with a couple of the tour security guards, Bobby was still inside the camper.

OK, so be it. At least he's safe and sound.

We went in the house and acted like there was nothing strange at all about the fact that the star of the show had sequestered himself in an unheated camper parked in front of a nice, warm house.

He finally came out the next morning, walked in the front door, and said, "Nice place! Where is everybody?"

I informed him that the rest of the tour personnel were settled at a nearby hotel.

We'd put the team up at the Sea Crest Beach, which was a popular resort during the season but pretty empty at the end of October. In fact, the only other guests were a group of mah-jongg ladies.

"I want to stay with everyone else," Bobby said.

I should've known. Bobby had always been a down-to-earth guy, and that didn't change when he got famous. That's one thing I've always admired about him. He moved over to the Sea Crest that day, and stayed with the company for the duration of the tour. He may have been the "star," but the tour was like family to him, and he didn't want to miss a minute of family time.

THIRTEEN

"Rolling Thunder" Unleashed

We'd built in a week of rehearsal time at the Falmouth Inn conference center before our first show. The musicians, technicians, security team, administrative personnel, and everybody else had made it there on schedule. A few days into rehearsals, the poet Allen Ginsberg joined the tour to play triangle, write original poems for the daily newsletter, and serve as our moral compass.

Allen was kind of a moral beacon among his fellow Beats, always championing the underdog and promoting the causes of truth and justice. If he saw something that did not rise to his standards, he would speak up about it. Having him around made us feel as if the spirit of the sixties was alive and well and "flower power" bloomed on.

I got to know Allen pretty well over the course of the tour. He was a very empathetic character, very much in tune with others. If he sensed I was getting a little too aggressive, he'd tell me to tone it down. One time, I was going after Larry "Ratso" Sloman—the author of *Reefer Madness*, who was covering the tour for *Rolling Stone*—about something, and Ginsberg kicked me in the ass. If anyone else had done it, I'd have rearranged his molecules, but, because it was Allen, I took it as he meant it: *Calm down, Louie.*

Allen and I kept in touch through the years, and when he died, I arranged for a Chabad in Jerusalem to recite the Kaddish for him—the Jewish prayer for the dead. (It seemed fitting since one of his most celebrated works is a poem called "Kaddish," written in memory of his own mother.)

One day during the rehearsals, we were advised that all of our equipment had to be moved temporarily out of the hall, as the hotel had booked a mah-jongg tournament there. So be it. Most of the company was glad to have the day off. Bobby had his own ideas.

During a break in the tournament action, the hotel manager announced to the ladies that they were in for a special treat. He had booked two folk singers to entertain them: Bob Zimmerman and Allen Ginsberg. Bobby came out and played a few numbers on the piano. Allen accompanied him on triangle and read some poetry. The ladies listened, clapped politely, and got back to their tiles. I'm pretty sure not one of them had any idea who they'd just heard.

The day before our debut concert in Plymouth, Jerry Seltzer and his crew hit the pavement. Their job was to walk through town, stopping people and passing out handbills featuring photos of Bobby and Joan and the particulars of the gig. One young lady pushing a baby carriage glanced at the handbill and threw it back at Jerry.

"Who the hell are you trying to kid?" she said. "You're saying Bob Dylan is in town, playing a show, and we haven't heard about it on the radio?"

"We immediately realized we had a problem," Jerry recalled. "No one believed Dylan was going to be there! At that point, I knew I was right that this was the craziest thing I had ever been associated with."

Jerry decided he'd better call a radio station in Boston, say he lived in Plymouth, and describe the handbills that were being handed out.

"I thought your listeners would want to know that Bob Dylan and Joan Baez are going to be performing up here," he said.

After that, word traveled fast, and the next day, when we put the tickets on sale at the box office, the show sold out immediately.

Things began to get easier. Once people got wind of the fact that there was this crazy traveling Dylan show, they were on the lookout for signs of it. We continued to hand out the flyers everywhere we went, which would tip off the local radio stations, who would then blast out the news. The whereabouts of the "traveling vagabonds" became everybody's favorite guessing game, and Bobby's fans ate the whole thing up.

The shows were packed. Some of the less seasoned performers—Scarlet Rivera, in particular—had never played for such large crowds. On opening night, she was so nervous that Bobby had to talk her off the metaphorical ledge. Since she was overwhelmed by the idea of so many people staring at her, she decided to wear dark glasses and paint a talisman on her face. That was the genesis of the white face paint Bobby wore during numerous shows.

In Cambridge, the getup prompted a kid in the audience to shout, "Why are you wearing a mask?"

"So that you'll look beyond my face and hear the words!" Bobby shot back without missing a beat.

Behind the curtains, the carnival atmosphere persisted and a genuine camaraderie developed among the musicians. The way Scarlet remembers it, "I was not very social but I felt at ease with the super-laid-back drummer, Howie Wyeth, and Joni Mitchell—who was brilliant, of course, but always gracious and warm besides being inspiring in her artistry. Bob was protective and supportive of me as a budding artist, and showed it on numerous occasions."

Most of the time, everybody in the entourage mixed and mingled well. But there was this one time, early on in the tour, when a particularly persistent, sneaky, and annoying reporter from the *Village Voice* did not take our tour's security protocol seriously. The rule was that nobody from the press was to come to the hotel or approach any of the performers without making a formal request via the tour office. This guy was warned numerous times, but he kept coming around, harassing people. Finally, I had two security guys put him in one of our extra hotel rooms, had the phones turned off, and stationed security outside the door. He was virtually under house arrest.

Gary and Barry were worried that this could be construed as kidnapping.

"Nah," I insisted, "it's more like a free vacation!"

The guy had to learn to play by the rules, or pay the

consequences. Bobby thought the whole thing was funny. When we finally let the reporter go, he promised to stick to the rules from then on—and he did. We may have relied heavily on journalists to get the word out about the shows, but making sure the artists felt safe and happy was a serious matter.

Ratso Sloman was so impressed with "Rolling Thunder" that he decided to take Bobby up on his offer to follow the whole tour. He ended up being almost as irritating as the guy from the *Village Voice*, but he was also endearing and entertaining in his own New York street kind of way. So, one day, during a meeting with the security guys, I threw an idea at them.

"You know," I said, "Ratso has told us he's going to write a book about 'Rolling Thunder.' I want to give him a good and fitting ending for it. When we get back to New York, take him out to dinner, and when he isn't looking, slip a Mickey in his drink. Then haul him down to the harbor where the freight boats are, give one of the mates five hundred bucks, and put him on a freighter to Poland or anywhere in Eastern Europe. When he comes to on the high seas, I want him to find a note in his pocket reading, "Have a great trip. Love, Louie."

I was only half kidding, but I guess it's lucky for me that the guys always found an excuse not to get it done. I think they were afraid of going to jail.

After the first week of shows, things had been going so well that Bobby decided that all of the band members and performers could bring their wives, girlfriends, and dates with them—one at a time, I mean. Suddenly, the size of our troupe was more than a hundred people, and growing all the time.

Joni Mitchell came to see one of the early shows and ended up sitting in. Of course, the audience loved her, and she enjoyed the experience enough to stay for the rest of the tour. Other artists who joined us at various times included Arlo Guthrie, Gordon Lightfoot, Patti Smith, Ringo Starr, Van Morrison, and Bruce Springsteen.

There was a special energy that flowed through the tour that was unlike anything I'd ever experienced. Audiences felt it too; they knew they were seeing something very special over the course of those four-to-five-hour sets. The reviews were stellar, and the fact that the itinerary was a closely guarded secret kept the media buzzing.

A wide range of celebrated artists came to see the show, and Bobby invited a lot of them to join in and perform. He was playing a lot of his older songs, along with cuts from *Blood on the Tracks* and a few as-yet-unreleased ones from *Desire*. For me, a highlight of the show was when Bobby and Joan sang together. I also loved Bobby's acoustic numbers, whatever Joni decided to perform, and the encores when everyone came out and sang "This Land Is Your Land." Each show was unique, and each one was a musical happening.

One day after a sound check, Bobby and I were standing in an offstage hallway when some people passed by with tour badges.

"You know them?" Bobby asked.

"No," I laughed. "Don't you?"

We both shrugged. The tour was mushrooming.

A few weeks into things, while we were in Hartford, Connecticut, Ratso arranged for Kinky Friedman to get together with Bobby. I knew they'd met a few years earlier, and Kinky seemed to know a lot of the guys on "Rolling Thunder." He fit right into the mix of colorful characters. That night, late in the set, Bobby sent a song out "to anybody here from Texas," which was certainly a tip of the cowboy hat to Kinky. I had no doubt Bobby was thinking Kinky might join us for the second leg of "Rolling Thunder," scheduled for the following spring.

About a week later, we hit Montreal. Bobby knew that Ratso was acquainted with Leonard Cohen, so he asked him to invite Leonard to our gig—and sure enough, he showed up backstage with his own mini entourage. He arrived right after Joni's set. The two Canadians greeted each other warmly with hugs, and he called her "my little Joni."

We were all hoping Leonard would go out and sing a song or two, but he said he preferred to sit back and listen. That was A-OK with Bobby, who was appreciative that he'd shown up at all, and dedicated "Isis" to him that night.

I mentioned the daily newsletter that Chris O'Dell put together for us. In addition to the hotel and venue information the company needed, it included humor, gossip, poems, and even original songs. Reading through them now brings back the whole spirit of the tour. Below is one of my favorite bits, written by Chris (alias the Zebra Phantom). Here is an excerpt from May 14, 1976:

- - - - - - - THE PHANTOM SPEAKS - - - - - - -

I am going to deviate slightly from the never-serious newsletter and talk about something we can all relate to: touring. Being on the road.

What is touring? It's a business. It's exposure. To the artist, it's part of his gig. You're thrown into an environment that involves only a certain amount of people and they become your life. You eat, sleep, and drink with them. You depend on them for your moods. You become so close to each other that you actually become one person. "that's heavy!" I've never been on a tour where at the end everyone was glad to say good-bye and return to their "normal" way of life. It's a drastic change. No one said it would be easy.

I get tired and i get bored but when i know that i have done a really good job within the duties of my gig, I feel high. When the band does a good show, they feel high. There's nothing like it. I love being part of this type of energy. Everyone on this tour belongs on the road. We may be too close to realize it sometimes, but what we do turns us and many other people on.

The "rolling thunder review" is music (and magic) and we are going to "knock their lights out." (maybe we'll even knock our own out at the same time!)

See you later,
THE ZEBRA PHANTOM

- -

The end of the tour would be a benefit for Rubin "Hurricane" Carter at Madison Square Garden in New York—but before that, Bobby wanted to do a performance at Rahway State Prison in New Jersey, where Carter was incarcerated. When news of it got out, it was probably the only time in history that people wanted to *break in* to a prison.

The inmates were not the most receptive audience, which took Joni by surprise; she was used to connecting with audiences. Instead of letting it rattle her, the girl from Saskatchewan decided, *If you can't wow them, join them.* She jumped off the stage, went directly over to some female inmates who had been mimicking her, and said, "Give me a break!" Then—to the amazement of all of us, she started to dance. A handsome, young inmate came up and asked if he could dance with her, and she graciously accepted his invitation.

"What are you in for?" she asked him.

"Murder," he replied casually.

You won't see that on your usual tour.

Actress Candice Bergen joined us at Rahway, but she had to leave early and said she needed a ride to JFK. Could I arrange that for her?

I knew Tom Mooney, one of our key security guys, was just the man for this special assignment.

"Sure, boss, whatever you want," he replied when I asked him to take care of it, beaming a smile the size of the Grand Canyon. When he returned a couple hours later, he gave me a big hug and said he owed me forever for the chance to have some private time and a nice long chat with the very special Candice.

As I mentioned, the last show of "Rolling Thunder" was a benefit for the incarcerated fighter Rubin "Hurricane" Carter, the subject of Bobby's song "Hurricane." Bobby believed Rubin was innocent of the crime he'd been convicted of, and was passionate about his case. What better way to use his fame and influence than to call attention to Rubin's plight?

The event at the Garden—called "Night of the Hurricane"—made news everywhere; everyone wanted to participate, and every fan wanted a ticket. In between songs, Muhammad Ali spoke and added his support. Rubin spoke via telephone hookup from Rahway Prison. Between the music and the speeches, the audience was on fire.

Just a few months later, Hurricane was granted a new trial.

Speaking about "Rolling Thunder," Joan Baez once said, "This tour has integrity. This is because of Bob."

I agreed with her. Bobby has always had vision that transcends that of most people. Another one of the musicians—I wish I could remember who—said, "You know what makes Bob different? He sees the end of things. When the rest of us are into something, it's as if it's going to last forever. Dylan, he's in just as deep, but he knows it's not going to last."

One night, during "This Land Is Your Land," Bobby's mom, kids, wife, and Joan Baez were all onstage with him, singing and dancing.

"He is getting all his mysteries unwrapped," quipped Allen—ever the poet.

When the tour was over, Allen reflected on the particular magic of it.

"'Rolling Thunder,'" he said, "with its sense of community, is saying we should all get our act together and do it properly and well. Once you have a view of the right path, you have to travel that path. Having gone through his changes in the sixties and seventies, just like everybody else, Bob got his powers together for this show. He had all the different kinds of art he has practiced—protest, improvisation, surrealism, invention, electric rock and roll, solitary acoustic-guitar strumming, duet work with Joan and other people—all these different practices ripened and were useable in one single show. There was room for Mick Ronson and his very English kind of space-music rock, Joan and her sort of refined balladry, and Roger McGuinn with his West Coast-style rock. All these different styles turned out to be useable."

Nobody could have said it better.

FOURTEEN

But How Did You Like the Play, Mrs. Lincoln?

It was December of 1975, and the first incarnation of "Rolling Thunder" had just ended. One afternoon, Bobby and I were celebrating (or, at least Bobby was) in the bar of the Westbury Hotel on the Upper East Side. Bobby was throwing down Rémys and trying to goad me into drinking a beverage stronger than orange juice for a change.

"We pulled it off, Louie," he said. "Come on! Be a man."

Finally, I caved and ordered some vodka with my orange juice. I didn't want Bobby to have to celebrate alone, and what was the harm in one screwdriver?

At that point, I remembered that Gary was supposed to pick Sara up and then come collect us. Bobby had promised Sam Shepard that we'd attend opening night of his new play, *Geography of a Horse Dreamer*. Sam was every inch a cowboy, and Bobby looked like one too that day. He was wearing a long red coat that could have been on loan from the Marlboro Man, along with a white gaucho hat. And by this point, it was patently obvious that he was feeling no pain.

We settled our tab and managed to make our way to the lobby just as Gary pulled up in the red Caddie convertible. Bobby scrambled into the front next to Sara, and

I got into the backseat, which felt uncomfortable … until I realized I was sitting on Bob Neuwirth. We sorted it out, and the five of us drove down to the Manhattan Theatre Club for the show.

When we got there, I had a brief word with Sam, who seemed nervous as hell. The fact that Bobby was in the audience didn't exactly ease his mind.

"Great," he said, "Bob Dylan is here, along with every critic in New York."

"That's good, isn't it?" I said innocently.

"Yes," he said, "unless you're the captain preparing to go down with the ship."

I guess all artists experience nerves. I'd certainly seen my share of the phenomenon on the tour. And, indeed, the response to the first act seemed to indicate that the ship was taking on water. Some of the critics actually appeared to be sleeping.

"It's cadaver city," whispered Sam at one point.

The only discernible activity in the audience was Bobby furiously scribbling notes and jamming them into the pockets of his long red coat. From time to time he would nudge a nearby audience member and ask if he could borrow a pencil or pen.

During intermission, I tracked down Sam again and found him only mildly suicidal. Bobby seemed to have disappeared, and that wasn't making him feel any better. Suddenly, he bolted out into the foyer, and then returned a few seconds later.

"I found Bob," he said.

"Where was he?" I asked.

"In the lighting booth. He'd walked in there thinking it was the entrance to the theater."

"Well, at least he's still here," I said, well aware that Bobby was somewhat worse off for his long tenure at the hotel bar.

I corralled him back to our seats in time for the lights to go down again.

If the opening act was a snoozer, the second act offered those who came back from intermission more than they'd bargained for. As the main character was about to get shot up with a hypodermic syringe by a fat doctor, a familiar voice from somewhere in the house shouted, "WAIT A MINUTE!"

The audience sat up straight and looked around, wondering if this was part of the play, or what.

"WAIT A SECOND!" shouted the voice again—clearly Bobby's. "WHY'S HE GETTING THE SHOT? HE SHOULDN'T GET THE SHOT! THE OTHER GUY SHOULD GET IT. GIVE IT TO THE OTHER GUY!"

By this point, I had Bobby in a hammerlock and was trying to haul him back down into his seat.

"Shut the hell up, Bobby," Neuwirth kept snarling, but Bobby was still struggling. Sam paced the aisles in a ferret-like frenzy, but there was nothing he could do.

Being the professionals they were, the actors soldiered on as if nothing were happening, and Gary and I managed to hold Bobby down, though he continued to squirm like a cat. Eventually, the play reached what Sam had described as its "Sam Peckinpah" climax, with shotguns going off and ketchup-blood flying all over the stage.

Somehow, Bobby managed to break free, pop up, and shout, "I DON'T HAVE TO WATCH THIS! I DIDN'T COME HERE TO WATCH THIS!"

The critics were definitely awake now, and writing furiously on their notepads. At this point, Sam seemed almost appreciative of the distraction from the play. When I thought about it, I figured that Bobby had just taken the initiative to say what a lot of people in the audience were probably thinking but would never have the guts—the chutzpah—to articulate. It wasn't his finest performance ... but the Rémys had clearly played a supporting role. Bobby was pretty forthright at his best, and under the influence, he was downright irrepressible.

Sam respected Bobby—and, as a fellow artist, even respected his insistence on expressing himself in that way at that moment.

Throughout Bobby's outburst, Sara remained stoic, sitting calmly and gazing straight ahead like Queen Elizabeth II reviewing the Life Guard. I surmised that she didn't want to do anything that might cause the situation to escalate.

I made a last-ditch effort to pull Bobby back down into his seat again, and the two of us went tumbling over backward into the row behind us. *It's the perfect yin and yang,* I recall thinking. *Explosions on the stage matched by explosions in the audience.*

Professionals or not, the actors just couldn't keep going any longer, and they stood on the stage, gaping at the ruckus.

At this point, Gary came over, smiling and offering us a hand so we could untangle ourselves and stand up.

"Is the play over?" he asked innocently.

I glanced around and saw a sea of confused faces, including those of the critics. I couldn't tell who knew it was Bob Dylan who'd caused the commotion, and who thought it was just some wild guy in a red coat and gaucho hat.

Bobby stumbled up the aisle looking for an exit, still shouting, "HE'S NOT SUPPOSED TO GET THE SHOT! THE OTHER GUY'S SUPPOSED TO GET THE SHOT!"

There's nothing like live theater.

FIFTEEN

Spirit Mountain

A couple nights after the adventure at the Manhattan Theatre Club, a few of us headed out to Brooklyn for Norman Mailer's annual Christmas party. Bob Neuwirth had an invitation, which he extended to Bobby, who, in turn, extended it to the rest of our traveling band of gypsies.

The party was truly a star-studded affair. Right away, I spotted Jackie O. and Joe Heller. Soon after we arrived, the "mentalist" and spoon bender Uri Geller asked Bobby to draw something on a piece of paper and keep it hidden. He said he was going to use telepathy to discover what Bobby had drawn—and he did it! I have no idea how, but Geller guessed Bobby had drawn a Star of David.

Gary Shafner was among our entourage that night, and he remembered a funny exchange between Joni and another guest.

"She [Joni] was talking to some New York socialite, the type of woman you'd expect to see at a Mailer soirée. They were having a pleasant conversation when the woman started to ask Joni questions like, *What do you do?* She didn't know who Joni was—and this was when she was a huge star! Joni politely replied that she was a musician. 'Oh, do you work on Broadway?' asked the woman, totally clueless. 'No … ' Joni said. It was really funny. Anyway, the interrogation went on and on like *What's My Line?*, with questions like, 'Have you ever made a record?' When she finally asked Joni her name—and got the answer— the woman was really embarrassed, but Joni was just so sweet about it."

Bobby and Mailer admired each other's work and talent. We were among the last to leave the party and when we finally left, in the early-morning hours, Mailer walked us out and thanked Bobby for coming. He didn't seem to mind that a few "plus-ones" had joined the festivities.

All things must end. The tour was over and I couldn't hang around, having misadventures in New York with Bobby anymore; I had to get back to "normal" life and my fish business. I wasn't alone in my reluctance to let go of the magic we'd created. Lots of the artists and crew expressed reluctance to go home, too.

"Well," I said to a bunch of them, "I'm going to Duluth. We have a great ski resort there called Spirit Mountain. Why don't you all come back to Duluth with me for a big old 'Rolling Thunder' group vacation?"

My all-access backstage badge for the "Rolling Thunder Revue" tour.

ROLLING THUNDER REVUE

SOLD OUT

We are sorry no tickets were available for you. There are no tickets at agencies or on the street. Any tickets that are being sold are probably counterfeit and will be refused admittance to the performance.   ...Thank you

The poster we had to have printed to let fans know there were no tickets left.

FLOOR
Retain Stub — Good Only

MON.
8:00 P.M.
DEC. 1
Davis Printing Limited

BOB DYLAN
PRICE -8.00 + RST .80 -$8.80
ADMIT ONE. Entrance by Main
Door or by Church Street Door.
Maple Leaf Gardens
LIMITED
CONDITION OF SALE
Upon refunding the purchase
price the management may
remove from the premises
any person who has obtained
admission by this ticket.
T   5 0

THE ROLLING THUNDER
REVUE
STARRING
BOB DYLAN
MON.   1975

5 CLUB   Forum   CLUB '65 CLUB
. Entrance   Entree rue CLOSSE
DEC.   DEC. 4

Adm. $7.72   8:00 $8.50
Tax   .78   P.M.

ROLLING THUNDER REVIEW
THU. EVE. - JEUDI SOIR - 8:00 P.M.

A 4 RANGEE
SIEGE
D. ENGLISH & CO. LTD. MTL.
Tax included
$8.50
Taxe incluse

MADISON
SQUARE
GARDEN

MON. EVE.
DEC. 8
1975

1st PROM $12.50

6

Night of the
Hurricane!

Rolling Thunder
Revue

TICKET
115 J 4
SEC. ROW SEAT

HARTFORD CIV
Hartford, Con

NOV
24
1975

Mon.
R
T

ADMISS

ROLLING THUNDER
REVUE

ROLLING THUNDER
REVUE
BOB DYLAN
JOAN BAEZ · JACK ELLIOT
BOB NEUWIRTH

COLISEE
SAMEDI EN SOIRÉE À 20h00
29 NOV. 1975 | **ROLLING THUNDER REVUE** | **29** NOV. 1975
Mezzanine $8.50

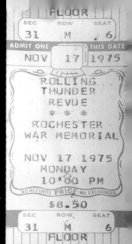

FLOOR
SEC 31 | ROW M | SEAT 6
ADMIT ONE
NOV 17 1975
THIS DATE
ROLLING THUNDER REVUE
* * *
ROCHESTER WAR MEMORIAL
NOV 17 1975
MONDAY
10:00 PM
NO REFUNDS PRICE NO EXCHANGES
$8.50
SEC 31 | ROW M | SEAT 6
FLOOR

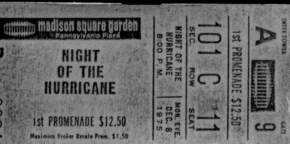

madison square garden
Pennsylvania Plaza
NIGHT OF THE HURRICANE
1st PROMENADE $12.50
Maximum Broker Resale Prem. $1.50

101 SEC. | C ROW | 11 SEAT
1st PROMENADE $12.50
A GATE 9
NIGHT OF THE HURRICANE 8:00 P.M.
MON. EVE. DEC. 8 1975

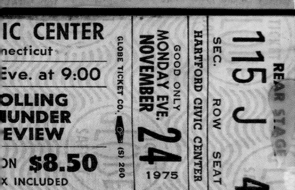

IC CENTER
nnecticut
Eve. at 9:00
OLLING THUNDER EVIEW
ON $8.50
X INCLUDED

GLOBE TICKET CO.
(S) 260

GOOD ONLY MONDAY EVE. NOVEMBER **24** 1975
HARTFORD CIVIC CENTER

115 SEC. | J ROW | 4 SEAT
REAR STAGE

ROLLING THUNDER REVUE

NAME: LOU KEMP
AUTHORIZED SIGNATURE:

© Louis Kemp Collect

These three shots were taken on October 23, 1975, at the "Rolling Thunder" pre-tour show at Gerde's Folk City—where Bob had been discovered . . .

. . . It was the owner Mike Porco's sixty-first birthday and Bob paid his respects by performing with Joan Baez, Phil Ochs, and many others.

. . . With us in this photo is Phil on the right.

All Photos by Mary Alfieri

The receipt for the winter clothing and ski accessories Bobby and Joan Baez had to buy when they came to visit me at Spirit Mountain.

SPIRIT VALLEY SKI & SPORT
5702 GRAND AVENUE
DULUTH, MINNESOTA 55807
PHONE: 218-624-7577

Customer's Order No. _____ Date: Dec. 22 1975

Name: Dylan & Baez

Address:

SOLD BY: SW   CASH   C.O.D.   CHARGE: X   ON ACCT.   MDSE. RETD.   PAID OUT

QUAN.	DESCRIPTION	PRICE	AMOUNT
1	Swing West Ens (Mauve)	49 95 ea	99 90
1	" " Jacket	✓	49 95
1	White Stag Jumpsuit	✓	66 00
1	" " Sweater		36 00
1	CB Jacket		69 00
1	Anba Stop		245 00
1	Sweater		29 90
1	Anba Kiss		245 00
1	Anba Sweater		50 00
1	hat		8 50
3	pom hats		33 00
2	underwear		18 00
1	after ski boot		85 00
2	" " "	23 90	47 80

All claims and returned goods MUST be accompanied by this bill.

TAX

2426 Received By

TOTAL 1083 05

GS-58   COMMUNITY BUSINESS & PRINTING SERVICE · DULUTH, MINN. 55802 50082-5

COLEL CHABAD
RABBI MEIR BAAL HANES CHARITIES IN THE HOLY LAND
UNDER THE AUSPICES OF THE LUBAVITCHER REBBE,
RABBI MENACHEM M. SCHNEERSON

כולל חב"ד
לצדקת רבי מאיר בעל הנס בארץ הקודש ת"ו
בנשיאות כ"ק אדמו"ר מליובאוויטש,
רבי מנחם מענדל שניאורסאהן

806 EASTERN PARKWAY, BROOKLYN, NY 11213 718-774-5446 FAX: 718-773-1614 • 5 HACHNASAT ORCHIM ST., P.O.B. 5046, JERUSALEM, ISRAEL

March 13, 2017

*** YAHRZEIT REMINDER ***

The Yahrzeit of your late beloved
Allen Ginsburg
is on 5 Nisan 5777, which corresponds to Saturday, April 1, 2017.
Yahrzeit observance begins Friday, March 31, 2017 at sundown.

Mr. Louis E Kemp

166904*1

www.colelchabad.org   Your contribution is tax deductible. Tax ID #11-3254483   info@colelchabad.org
TWO CENTURIES OF HELPING THE NEEDY OF ISRAEL IN A MANNER WHICH SUSTAINS THEIR SELF ESTEEM

I still receive an annual yahrzeit (anniversary of his passing) reminder for Allen Ginsburg, for whom I arranged a special kaddish—prayer for the dead—to be said at Chabad in Jerusalem in perpetuity.

Hanging out at Spirit Mountain after "Rolling Thunder" (clockwise from top left): me, Joan Baez, Bobby, and my sister Sharon.

Joan Baez and Bob performing in Providence, Rhode Island, during the "Rolling Thunder Revue" tour. I'm standing about ten or twelve feet behind them, but the angle makes it look like I'm a lot closer. *Photo by Mary Alfieri*

Joan Baez gave me this photo in which she shows off the fun and playful side of her that few people knew. On the mat, she wrote, "Hey Looey, I need to explain to you that I have another lifestyle … that's ok … I'm flexible … wanna buy me a Mercedes Benz? Love, Joan."

BILL GRAHAM

October 30, 1974

Lou Kemp
4832 W. Superior Street
Duluth, Minn.

Dear Lou:

A brief note to thank you for the fish. I've st an all-time
whitefish eating record, having must consumed my seventeenth
whitefish breakfast in succession. My fins are looking irregu-
lar, but very smart.

Again, my thanks. Hope you and yours are in good health and
in good spirits.

Cheers,

Bill Graham

BG:mg

201-11TH STREET SAN FRANCISCO, CA. 94103 PHONE (415) 864-0815 TELEX 34256

Bill Graham and I became friends over the years. He loved the smoked
trout from A. Kemp Fish Company so much that we arranged a trade:
I sent him fish whenever he wanted it, and he provided me with
concert tickets.

It might surprise you to learn that a lot of them were game. So I got on the phone with Spirit Mountain and reserved all the bungalows I could get. Then I warned my mother we might be having some houseguests for a night or two.

Bobby, Sara, and their kids decided to come, along with Joan Baez and her son; Roger McGuinn; Barry Imhoff; Gary Shafner; our tour photographer, Ken Regan; and some others.

Once we hit town, Bobby, Gary, and I went to the Army-Navy store downtown to buy cold-weather clothes for everybody. None of them was equipped for the kind of cold that accompanies a Duluth winter. Like most "North Countryers," Bobby and I were decent skiers. Some of the others were newbies, but willing to give it a try.

We skied during the day and hung out in the chalet at night, frolicking, partying, dancing, singing, and drinking. Everyone seemed happy to extend our time together by a few more days.

One day, walking up to the chalet after a particularly good run, Bobby and I ran into a great friend and partner in one of my companies, Jeno Paulucci. Bobby and Jeno had traveled opposite paths in life. Bobby had been born in Duluth and moved to Hibbing, while Jeno had been born in Hibbing and moved to Duluth. Bobby had left the North Country to make his mark on the world, while

Jeno had stayed behind to build his one-hundred-million-dollar Chun King food empire.

Despite their differences in trajectory, the two shared the title of the area's most famous and successful sons. Both were risk-takers and knew how to think outside of the box. They had a good time sharing memories of Hibbing, but at some point, Jeno told Bobby he needed me back at our business; there was a great opportunity to expand into Central America, and I'd have to fly south to evaluate the business. Jeno knew we were done with the tour, but Bobby said he needed me for another phase of "Rolling Thunder." Naturally, this piqued my curiosity.

I have to say, I enjoyed it a little, being fought over by these two super-successful guys.

"Don't worry, gentlemen," I said. "I'm sure I can handle both things!"

Turned out, I could.

The only minor blemish on the whole trip was when my mother threw Roger McGuinn and my sister out of the house on one of the coldest days of the year, after catching them smoking pot in the basement. They went to a neighbor's house and called a taxi to take them to Spirit Mountain, where they were generously given some blankets and room on the floor in one of the bungalows.

The next day, Roger was still shivering and my mother Frieda was still shouting, "There will be no doing drugs in this house!" Take it from me, she knew how to dole out tough love. Bobby found the incident highly amusing.

One night, we all decided to go to a very popular restaurant in town, the Chinese Lantern, for dinner, and I brought my mother along. We commandeered a big table in the middle of the dining room and she sat proudly in the seat of honor, surrounded by celebrities. A lot of her friends were eating there, and she smiled and waved at them like a queen surrounded by her subjects.

I was sitting directly across from Joan Baez, with whom I had a very friendly, jovial relationship. We often joked around and teased each other. I am not sure who started it, but somehow Joan and I got into a food fight, and, fierce competitors that we were, neither of us was willing to back off. Soon, food was flying all over the restaurant. I'm not proud to say that several blue-haired ladies at nearby tables ended up with chow mein highlights in their hair. My poor mother's pride turned to shame in an instant.

"Louis! Louis! Stop that!!" she pleaded as she and her friends watched in horror.

I looked over and saw that Bobby was laughing himself silly. I have no doubt that he would have joined in had Sara not been there.

Finally, when we'd exhausted our ammunition and ourselves, Joan and I called a truce. I waved the waiter over to bring us some fresh napkins and menus so we could order food to replace what we'd propelled around the room. I generally hate to waste food, but how many chances was I ever going to get to pelt Joan Baez with wontons?

Spirit Mountain had provided a fittingly joyous coda to the tour, and we all happily went our separate ways for the holidays. Meanwhile, "Rolling Thunder 2" was quietly gestating.

SIXTEEN

Yelapa to "Rolling Thunder 2"

One of the things somebody had come up with on the first leg of "Rolling Thunder"—for the amusement and edification of the company—was a "Rolling Thunder Review" daily newsletter. As I mentioned, Chris O'Dell wrote it, and I have a copy of every damn one of them. Here's a little excerpt from the April 22, 1976, issue:

- - - - - - - - - - ROLLING RAP - - - - - - - - - - -

Here's your chance to join the "in" group—the "I Hate Lou Kemp" Fan Club. For only $10, you receive a membership card, and "I Hate Lou Kemp" T-shirt, and an 8x10 glossy of Lou Kemp sitting on the toilet, mumbling about fish on the phone. Send cash only to Kinky Friedman, president of the "I Hate Lou Kemp" Fan Club, in care of this newspaper.

- -

On January 25, 1976, forty thousand people attended a second benefit concert for Hurricane Carter, held at the Houston Astrodome. In addition to Bobby and many of his "Rolling Thunder Revue" troupe, performers included Dr. John, Isaac Hayes, Stevie Wonder, and Ringo Starr.

Scarlet Rivera reminisced about the charter flight that carried us from L.A. to Houston.

"One special person on the plane was Ringo Starr," she recalled. "As I walked down the aisle, Ringo 'chatted me up,' as they say in England, and told me how much he liked the way I moved. I was a bit floored but replied, 'I hope you like the way I play too!'"

Since all of the artists had waived their fees for the benefit, Bobby had been kind enough to send them to the Nudie's Rodeo Tailors in L.A. before we left, to pick out a shirt or dress for the show. (In case you aren't familiar with Nudie Cohn, he was the guy who designed those rhine-stone-covered outfits for all the legendary country stars, rock stars, Elvis—everybody.) When the troupe came out on stage in Houston, it was an explosion of color and crazy patterns. Somehow, as much as everyone clashed, they all matched perfectly.

The concert was a huge success, packed with cheering fans who were thrilled to see so many of their idols on one stage. The next day we were supposed to go back to L.A. but Joni was on tour in the area, and asked Bobby to come to her concert in Dallas. Well ... she didn't just ask; she pushed pretty hard. Since she'd performed at all those "Rolling Thunder" concerts without ever asking to be paid, Bobby felt he owed her. He told her we'd be there.

Gary rented a car and he, Bobby, Kinky, and I headed for Dallas. But we got off to a late start, hit all kinds of traffic, and didn't get to the venue until just after the show ended. Joni was disappointed that Bobby had missed it, so she convinced him to come to her next one—in Austin.

Once again, he promised her he'd be there.

Since we'd set out from L.A. prepared for just a one-day trip, we had to take a time-out to shop for some shirts, socks, underwear, and other stuff. I canceled our flight from Dallas back to L.A., and late that afternoon, we hit the road to Austin. This time, Gary leaned on the gas to make sure we'd get to the concert on time.

In spite of Gary's bat-out-of-hell driving, it was starting to look like Groundhog Day: We were running late again. When Gary went flying through a speed trap, a Texas State Trooper chased us down and promptly arrested him. We followed the police car as he hauled Gary twenty miles away to face a judge and pay a fine. What else could we do?

Once the fine was paid, we got back on the road to Austin. Believe it or not, we made it to the show about halfway through, and to make up for all our lapses, Bobby walked onstage unannounced for the encore and sang a couple of songs. When the crowd realized who was standing up there, they went wild.

Backstage after the show, we ran into Dennis Hopper. He told Bobby he was going to Yelapa, Mexico, and described it as a great, relaxing, beautiful place.

"Want to come along?" he asked.

"Sounds good," said Bobby. "What do you think, Louie?"

What do you *think* I thought?

"Let's do it!" I said.

Everybody knows Dennis was an accomplished actor,

filmmaker, photographer, and artist. He also happened to be a good guy and a lot of fun to be with.

Austin being Kinky Friedman country, the entire gypsy caravan left Joni's concert and went to Kinky's parents' house for a barbecue. They had a large deck in the backyard, and everybody was hanging out smoking pot and drinking. Inside, Bobby and Joni snuck off to play a mini concert in Kinky's little sister's bedroom. Everyone was in high spirits.

I have a very poignant memory of that evening. Kinky's dad, Tom Friedman, had invited a colleague named Warren to stay with them. He was battling cancer and was too ill to join the party, so he retired to one of the back bedrooms. I overheard someone say that Warren really wanted to meet Bobby, so I tried to find him, but couldn't track him down in the crowded house. Joni got wind of the situation and, without saying a word about it, went into the bedroom and played Warren a song or two. He was very moved by her gesture, and so was I.

The next day it was back to the store to buy more clothes, and once again cancel our plane tickets to L.A. Bobby, Kinky, Gary, and I drove to San Antonio to meet Dennis and take off for Puerto Vallarta, the closest airport to this Garden of Eden he'd told us about.

The only way to get in or out of Yelapa was aboard a boat called *The Sombrero*, formerly owned by John Wayne. It was a festive ride, complete with a mariachi band playing traditional Mexican music. My first view of Yelapa was of a beautiful bay bordered by a pristine sandy beach. Dennis told us that the movie *The Night of the Iguana*, with Richard Burton and Ava Gardner, was shot right at that spot.

Set in a beautiful cove, Yelapa was tiny; only two hundred people lived there, and it had no roads, cars, or electricity. Its only hotel was right on the beach and powered by a generator that shut off at eight o'clock each night.

It turned out that Benny Shapiro, an old friend of Bobby's who'd had a club on the Sunset Strip back in the day, had a house in Yelapa. Bobby and Dennis decided to stay with Benny, while Kinky, Gary, and I stayed in little huts at the hotel. Our accommodations were just as Dennis had described: simple, relaxing, and beautiful. It was the perfect soft landing after all those months on the road.

The hotel had a gift shop, and, since we'd arrived unprepared for a beach vacation, I bought myself a white ruffled shirt, string-tied pants, flip-flops, and a large sombrero. I put on the whole getup and went down to the beach— where I promptly fell asleep in a hammock with the sombrero over my face.

When Bobby came down from Benny's to look for me, the desk clerk told him I was at the beach. He walked around for a while, but, of course, he didn't spot me in my "disguise," so he went back and asked again. The clerk reassured him I was down there. Bobby looked again. No Louie.

Finally, the desk guy said, "Follow me," and led Bobby back to the beach. He walked over to my hammock, pointed at me, and said, "That is your friend."

Bobby lifted the sombrero from my sleepy face and smiled.

"It didn't take you long to go native," he said.

I squinted up at him and replied, "I'm no longer a gringo, like you," and we both laughed.

To Bobby's delight, not one of the two hundred locals knew or cared who he was. He played chess with me, Kinky, and random people in the marketplace. He painted a lot. One day on the beach, he tossed a pair of cowboy boots into the air and painted them exactly as they fell.

More significantly, Bobby wrote. Everywhere we went, I saw him writing on scraps of paper, napkins, menus, matchbook covers. Finding himself neither home nor on the road, Bobby was inspired.

It was in Yelapa that I really got to know Kinky. One day, as we lay in adjacent lounge chairs under a beach umbrella, he told me about meeting Bobby.

"I met Bob in 1973," he began. "And it might sound trite, but I felt like I'd known him my whole life. Before that, listening to his music, I'd always suspected one day we'd be friends—but I never thought it would seem like a Hollywood dream sequence."

I closed my eyes and listened as he continued.

"The Texas Jewboys and I had just wrapped up our first West Coast show at the Troubadour in L.A., and Bob came upstairs to our little dressing room. This gesture was appreciated by everybody, though his wardrobe did raise a few eyebrows: Bob was barefoot and wearing a long white robe. We talked a little in the hallway and he mentioned some of the songs he liked from my set, including, 'Ride 'em Jewboy.'

"A couple of weeks later, at midnight, my road manager, Dylan Ferrero, and I were waiting at Santa Monica Pier for a baby-blue Cadillac convertible to pick us up and take us to a rendezvous with Bob. Soon, we were speeding through the fragrant California night, up to Malibu, to Roger McGuinn's house. When we got there, there were a few people scattered around inside, including my Nashville buddy, Kris Kristofferson.

"Kris ushered us to the kitchen and there was Bob, sitting on the counter with a bottle of wine in one hand and a guitar in the other. By way of introduction, he sang a near-perfect version of 'Ride 'em Jewboy.' When he finished, I said, 'So … now am I supposed to play one of yours?'"

Although Yelapa was one big tropical beach, I rarely saw Bobby when he wasn't wearing his heavy, black leather jacket. Kinky said he must feel a chill that nobody else can feel. I think maybe he just liked wearing that jacket.

I'd heard that Kinky had been a chess prodigy from the age of seven. He and Bobby played a lot of chess while in Yelapa, and this led to one of the more memorable events of the trip. The local chess champ challenged Kinky to a game in the public marketplace at high noon. Kinky showed up in full cowboy regalia, wearing a big, black cowboy hat; black pants and boots; and a sparkling "Jesus coat" that Bobby had bought at Nudie's and given to him.

Word had gotten around about the match, and many locals were betting on their homegrown champion to beat the gringo. Had Kinky gotten in over his head?

"Are you sure you were a child prodigy?" I asked him.

"Hell, yes," he said. "I played Samuel Reshevsky, the grand master of the world, when I was seven. Of course, it's been downhill from there."

So, I bet $200 on Kinky and kept my fingers crossed. Just before the match was to begin, Bobby showed up, and I told him what I'd done.

He walked straight over to the guy who was holding the money, and said, "I'll take half of Louie's action."

Kinky won!

I stayed in Yelapa for two weeks, other than a couple of quick trips on *The Sombrero* to Puerto Vallarta, where I could make a few calls. It wasn't easy trying to run my fish business from the middle of nowhere, but I was determined to try.

Kinky left around the time I did, but Bobby, Dennis, and Gary stayed in Mexico for another two months. Yelapa affects everybody differently, but whether you stay for two days, two weeks, or two months, something about the place takes root inside you.

Thirty years after that trip, I was at a program at my daughter's school, and who did I see but Dennis Hopper. Turns out his son went there too. Dennis recognized me immediately and, after giving me a big hug, introduced me to his wife.

"This is Louie Kemp," he said. "Bob, Louie, and I were in Yelapa together."

She smiled and said, "I know all about it, Dennis. I've heard that story many times."

After Yelapa, it was back to work on both my business and "Rolling Thunder." The spring tour was set to kick off on April 18, 1976, after a week of rehearsals in Lakeland, Florida. Kinky, Dennis, and Donna Weiss were new additions to our gypsy caravan. Jack Elliott, Allen Ginsberg, Ronee Blakley, and Sam Shepard were sitting this phase out, but Mick Ronson, Scarlet Rivera, Roger McGuinn, Joan Baez, and most of the band were back on board. When Joan showed up, she'd cut her trademark long hair short. When I asked her about it, she said, "I figured Bobby and you liked long hair better, so ... "

Unlike the previous leg of the tour, which had taken us to smaller venues and civic centers, the spring gigs were in stadiums and large arenas. Thanks to our amazing crew, touring with "Rolling Thunder" was like living at the top of the food chain. We'd leave our luggage in our rooms, and the next day, it would magically appear in the hotel in the next city. If a guitar string broke in the middle of a set, the best and fastest guitar techs in the world would have it replaced and tuned up before the performer had time to miss a beat.

As we swung through the South, the ambience seemed friendlier and more colorful. Some of this was cultural, but our little getaway to Yelapa hadn't hurt either. The whole carnival atmosphere had become so comfortable that it no longer seemed strange to see adult artists walking around in face paint, elaborate costumes, and turbans.

One of the more memorable shows was toward the end of the tour, at Hughes Stadium in Fort Collins, Colorado. It had been a pretty miserable morning. We had a big film crew from NBC there to tape the concert, but the rain just would not let up. I paced around, nervous that the whole thing would be a washout. But when I looked out at the crowd forming in front of the stage, I could see that everyone was having a blast! They were sliding around in the mud and dancing in the rain. By the time Bobby took the stage, the rain had slowed to a drizzle and the energy was electric.

Two days later, in Salt Lake City, we played our last gig. The morning after I was still sleeping when Joan came by my room to say good-bye on her way to the airport.

"But we're just getting to know each other," I said.

She just laughed, gave me a kiss on the cheek, and left.

Joan and I had spent enjoyable and fun times together, but ultimately our relationship deteriorated. I think she surmised—correctly—that my first loyalty would always be to Bobby.

SEVENTEEN

"The Last Waltz"

Bill Graham was a big fan of the smoked Lake Superior trout I had introduced him to while we were on "Tour '74." From time to time, he would ask me if he could buy some from me, but, of course, I said there was no way I'd sell it to him.

He didn't feel right about taking it for free, so he said, "Let's make a deal. How about you send me the smoked trout, and I'll give you concert tickets whenever you want?"

"Deal."

When the Rolling Stones played Minneapolis, he gave me the best seats in the house. And when he was planning The Band's final concert, to be called "The Last Waltz," he contacted me. It went without saying that I'd be at the show ... but that wasn't what the call was about. He told me The Band was planning a Thanksgiving feast at the venue, prior to the concert. Would I provide some salmon for it?

"Sure," I said. "Consider it a gift from me and Bobby."

True to my word, I provided three hundred pounds of Alaskan king salmon for the "Last Waltz" feast, compliments of the boys from the North Country.

The day before the concert, Bobby and I flew up to San Francisco. We had booked rooms at the Miyako Hotel, where a lot of the concert people were staying. We agreed to meet up in the lobby and go over to Winterland together for the show.

At the appointed time, I went down to meet Bobby but he wasn't there yet, so I looked around for a place to wait. I spotted an empty chair next to a distinguished-looking black man. We greeted each other and, after a little while, Bobby came down. He saw me and started in my direction, and when he was about ten feet away, he started laughing. I went over to meet him, and as we walked toward the door, Bobby was still chuckling.

"That," he said, "is one of the funniest sights I've ever seen."

"What?" I asked innocently.

"Muddy Waters and Louie Kemp sitting together."

"That was Muddy Waters?"

Who knew?

Winterland was quite a scene. Bill had decorated the hall spectacularly, borrowing sets from *La Traviata*. There were tables with mountains of delicious-looking food, including the salmon we'd provided. The show had sold out in one day, and the place was brimming with 5,400 fans.

Today, thanks in no small part to Martin Scorsese's epic film of the event, everybody knows who played at that concert. Among others (and aside from The Band), there was Neil Young, Neil Diamond, Joni Mitchell, Van Morrison, Muddy Waters, Paul Butterfield, Eric Clapton, Ringo Starr, Bobby Charles, Ronnie Hawkins, Dr. John,

Stephen Stills, Ron Wood, and, last but definitely not least, Bobby—the musician's musician.

It seemed that all of the artists wanted to talk to Bobby, and he was friendly and gracious to everyone. Governor Jerry Brown was backstage and took the opportunity to fawn over him. Bobby just remained Bobby—laid back and taking it all in.

In order to get his film bankrolled, Scorsese had had to promise a "headliner." When he'd dropped Bob's name, Warner Bros. had quickly forked over the cash on the understanding that Bobby would be a highlight of the film.

At the time, Bobby was editing the movie we'd shot during "Rolling Thunder," *Renaldo and Clara*. Bobby's appearance in the Scorsese film concerned Howard Alk, who was working with Bobby on the editing and development of that project. Would Bobby's appearance in *The Last Waltz* detract from the impact of their own movie?

Bobby thought about this, and just before the concert began, he gave Bill Graham an ultimatum.

"I don't want all of my songs to be filmed," he said. "Just two of them. I'm going to put Louie on the stage next to you and Marty. He will tell you when you can film me."

Bill freaked out.

"Our financing depends on your appearance in this film!" he insisted.

But Bobby would not relent. He was planning to perform four songs, and they could film only the last two.

There I stood, "the enforcer," next to Marty, Bill, and Jonathan Taplin, the producer. The cameramen took their marching orders from Scorsese, of course, but I was tasked with getting them to turn their cameras away from Bobby and come down from their towers during his early numbers. After that, they could scamper back up and shoot as they pleased.

What could possibly go wrong?

The lights went down and Bobby came out to a thundering ovation. He danced around the stage as he performed a lively, rousing rendition of "Baby, Let Me Follow You Down." The crowd went wild. Then he moved right into "Hazel" from *Planet Waves*. Near the end of it, I told Bill and Marty to get ready, and signaled the cameramen to get back on their perches and swing their cameras around.

The cameras rolled as Bobby launched into his third song, "I Don't Believe You (She Acts Like We Never Have Met)," and kept going through his fourth, "Forever Young." That one really brought down the house.

That was supposed to be the end of the set, but Bobby calls his own shots, and he decided to swing back into "Baby, Let Me Follow You Down"—much to the surprise of everybody, including The Band. When I realized what was happening, I told Marty and Bill to turn off the cameras.

Marty pretended he didn't hear me, and Bill went completely bonkers.

"Screw you!" he shouted. "Roll the damn cameras. Roll them!"

Right there, as Bobby was performing, Bill and I got into a yelling and shoving match.

"Back off!" Bill screamed. "This is history, man! Don't mess with it. This is my show!"

I understood where Bill was coming from. I knew him to be a volatile guy, accustomed to controlling everything in his universe. He resented Bobby and me telling him what he could or could not do at his own show. But I had a job to do and I was trying like hell to do it.

The uproar caused Bobby to glance over at me like, *What the hell's going on?* Then he went back to hypnotizing the audience with his artistry as I continued trying to fend off Bill and shut down the camera crew.

By the time Bobby gave the crowd yet another gift by performing "I Shall Be Released," along with The Band and a bunch of other artists, I'd given up trying to stop the inevitable. After the show, I explained to Bobby what had happened.

In his usual fashion, he said, "It's OK, Louie. You did a good job."

EIGHTEEN

My Seder with Bobby and Brando

I have always believed that Bobby was the Marlon Brando of music, and Marlon was the Bob Dylan of acting. I'm proud to say I'm the guy who brought them together at a Passover Seder.

This rather cosmic situation came about in the midseventies, when I was spending some time in L.A. With some difficulty, I had managed to make reservations for my sister, a few friends, and myself to attend Seder at a synagogue in Hollywood. The event was sold out, and the ladies in charge were mildly irritated when I called back several times to try to add names. Just hours before the service, I got a call from Marlon.

"Hey, Louie, how about joining me for dinner tonight?"

"Can't do it, Marlon," I said. "It's Passover, and I'm going to Seder at a synagogue."

"Passover!" he said. "I've always wanted to attend a Seder. Can I come with?"

How could I refuse Don Corleone, Stanley Kowalski, and Colonel Kurtz all rolled into one? Besides all that, I knew Marlon to be a mensch and a genuine friend of the Jews.

I already told you about how I got to know Marlon—
through his son Christian, who'd worked for me. In the
mid-seventies, whenever I found myself in L.A., Marlon
and I would get together. It was around that time that I
was starting to take my religion more seriously, and we
talked about Judaism. Marlon told me, with great pride
and satisfaction, about his support for Israel even before
it became a state. He explained that in 1946, two years
before Israel achieved statehood, he'd desperately believed
that the survivors of the Holocaust deserved to have their
own land, free from anti-Semitic tyranny.

"People who have fought so hard to survive need and
deserve their own land," he proclaimed.

He also told me he believed his success in theater and
movies was largely due to some Jewish people in New
York who had befriended and taught him. In particular, he
singled out Stella Adler, the legendary acting coach who
had both taught and housed Marlon while he was getting
on his feet as an actor. He was proud of the fact that he
could converse in Yiddish, having learned it while living
with Stella and her family. To prove that he was on the
level, he spoke a few phrases of Yiddish to me and waited
for me to respond.

"Marlon, I can't speak Yiddish. My parents never taught
me any. I guess they didn't want me to know what they
were saying to each other."

"What kind of Jew are you that you can't speak Yiddish!" he said, laughing. "I'm a better Jew then you are!"

It wasn't the only thing Marlon could do that I couldn't.

So, you can see why I had to find Marlon a seat at that Seder. I called the temple and—without saying who it was for—pleaded with them to add just one more name to the list.

A short time later, Marlon called me back and asked if he could bring a friend.

"Of course," I said, and called the temple again.

The ladies were pretty sick of me at this point, but somehow I got them to agree to squeeze just one more person in. This was absolutely the last one, they told me. They were officially sold out—even for Louie Kemp.

I'd barely hung up the phone when Bobby called. When I told him about the Seder, he asked if he and Sara could join us.

I gulped and dialed the synagogue's number yet again, which, at that point, I had memorized. I felt like Moses standing in front of the pharaoh as I tried to soften the heart of that reservation lady—but somehow I managed it, and without using Bobby's name.

It was worth it.

The Seder was surreal, to say the least. Bobby, clad in typical black leather jacket and jeans, sat to my right, and Marlon, to my left. His guest was Native American activist Dennis Banks, of Wounded Knee fame, in full regalia and looking like he was ready to attack General Custer at a moment's notice.

The service progressed normally for a while, with only the occasional odd glance from someone at another table—and who could blame them? Marlon was one of the most famous faces in Hollywood, and looked quite capable of breaking into a spontaneous rendition of "Stel-la!!!" at any moment.

Just as I was immersing myself in the story of the Jews' enslavement in Egypt, Bobby leaned toward me and whispered, "What gives with Marlon?"

I glanced to my left and noticed that Marlon's face had turned an unusual shade of chartreuse.

"Are you OK, Marlon?" I said.

No answer.

"Is he OK?" Bobby persisted.

Finally, Marlon croaked, "Yeah," as he gulped a large glass of water. "I ate a bunch of the white stuff."

He pointed toward a large bowl of *chazeret*, which is Hebrew for the Jewish people's greatest contribution to mankind: horseradish. As was his custom, Marlon had sampled it with gusto. Bobby and I tried hard to look serious, but we ended up dissolving in laughter—thus drawing the attention of the rabbi leading the service.

"Mr. Brando," he said, "would you please do us the honor of reading the next passage from the Haggadah?"

"It would be my pleasure," said Marlon, recovering his composure and smiling broadly. He stood up and, as the crowd of three hundred sat spellbound, delivered the passage as if he were performing Shakespeare on Broadway. Any rabbi in the world would've coveted the intensity with which they watched and listened to Marlon. When he finished, you could tell they wanted to applaud, but knew it was inappropriate. They applauded anyway.

Later in the service, the rabbi singled out another member of our party.

"Mr. Dylan," he said. "Would you do us the honor of singing a song?"

Even as the rabbi produced an acoustic guitar, I knew from my long association with Bobby that this was not going to happen. He would respectfully decline, or leave it to me to deliver the bad news. Just as I was leaning in to ask him if he wanted me to handle it, Bobby stood up and made his way across the room, toward the little stage. The assembled worshippers seemed as shocked and surprised as I was.

What will he play? I wondered. *Maybe "The Times They Are A-Changin"... or, better yet, "With God on Our Side"?*

Wrong on both counts.

The rabbi handed Bobby the guitar, and he walked up to the microphone with the confidence of a maestro. He proceeded to perform a beautiful acoustic version of "Blowin' in the Wind." When the last chord had reverberated off the walls, the temple rang with applause and cheers.

At the conclusion of the service, it seemed that everybody in the place wanted to stop by our table to shake hands with Bobby and Marlon. To their credit, both of them hung around till the bitter end. At one point, a little blonde girl of about six tugged at Bobby's sleeve and pointed to her autograph book. She then put her hands together in the internationally recognized gesture that translates to *Pleeeeeeease sign my autograph book or I will cryyyyyy.* Bobby beamed her a big smile and signed. Even the ladies who'd given me the business for calling so many times stopped by to express their gratitude.

"Thanks for letting my people go," I quipped.

Many years later, I was sitting at my desk in my Minnesota office when my secretary came in to inform me there was a man on the phone claiming to be Marlon Brando.

"If he says he's Marlon Brando, he probably is," I told her, and she put him through.

Marlon and I had a nice chat, during which he said he'd been thinking about the time I took him to the Seder, and how much he had enjoyed it.

"Any group of people who gather together once a year— all over the world—to thank God and celebrate an event that took place more than 3,500 years ago, they're pretty inspiring to me," he said. "I just wanted to tell you … I was honored to be a part of it."

NINETEEN

Nobody Beats the Bear

An indicator of what kind of manager Albert Grossman was going to be came in the mid-sixties, after a mutual friend had taken Bobby to Andy Warhol's studio in New York, known as the Factory. Andy was a big fan of Bobby's and gave him one of his life-size silkscreens, the one called *Double Elvis*.

That piece is well known and widely reproduced nowadays, but Bobby wasn't wild about it. Perhaps that's why he and his pal Bob Neuwirth, attached it to the roof of his station wagon and drove to Woodstock with it flapping like a banner. (To be fair, at the time Bobby was only a few years removed from Hibbing and not very tuned in to the art world.)

Grossman, on the other hand, knew what an original Warhol was worth. So, when Bobby told him that he needed a sofa, Grossman was more than happy to give him one of his old ones—in exchange for *Double Elvis*.

Cut to the early eighties, when Bobby and I were living together in a house in Brentwood. We'd often hang out in the kitchen, drinking, eating, and talking about what we were up to. On one occasion I could tell he was aggravated about something.

When I asked him what was wrong he said, "They want me to sign more papers."

"Who does?" I asked.

"Albert Grossman, my ex-manager from back in the sixties," he said. "The guy took a huge percentage of the earnings from my songs and publishing back in the day, and now he wants me to sign more papers."

"What does your lawyer say about that?"

"He says I should sign them. That you can't fight Albert."

That sounded like terrible advice.

After a little digging, I figured out why this attorney was urging Bobby to sign the papers. The guy represented Grossman as well!

This is crazy, I thought. Clearly, it was a major conflict of interest.

But Bobby persisted in thinking he had no choice.

"Nobody's ever beaten Albert," he kept saying, dispirited.

For a guy who was as brave and brilliant as anybody I'd ever met, he could be very naïve about things. In all the time he'd been managed by Grossman, he'd never read any of his contracts; he'd trusted the man completely.

"Don't sign anything, Bobby!" I implored. "This is outrageous and illegal. I'm going to get you a great attorney who'll be on *your* side. Not only will we stop this nonsense, we're going to get your rights back."

The lawyer I had in mind was Frank Berman, an old fraternity brother of mine from U Minn., who'd stayed a close friend ever since. Frank was based in the Twin Cities—not a big New York lawyer or Hollywood hotshot. He didn't even specialize in entertainment law. But I knew Frank was a tenacious, brilliant attorney who was not afraid of anything or anyone. I thought of him as a cross between Rocky and Alan Dershowitz.

I gazed across the kitchen table at my forlorn-looking friend, who was still mumbling, "No one has ever beaten the Bear." Well, Frank Berman could beat the damn Bear. At least, I hoped he could, because Bobby was counting on me. It was one thing to fix a friend up on a bad blind date, but this was something else. This was war, and if we were going to start it, we'd better win.

It turned out that Frank had recently moved to L.A., so a few days later, he came to the house. When Bobby and I explained the situation, Frank looked like the back of his head was going to blow off.

"You can't have the same attorney represent both parties in forming a contract!" he said. "And he took an extremely high percent of your rights. Get me all the documents you have since the beginning of your association with Grossman. Let me study them, and we'll have another meeting."

Bobby arranged to have all the documents sent to Frank's office. He reviewed them quickly and studied up on the applicable law. Then he called me.

"This is a complete disgrace," he said. "He's got to fight this."

When we met again, Frank reiterated to Bobby that the whole thing was outrageous—a blatant conflict of interest. The terms of the contract were onerous.

"They took advantage of your age and lack of business experience," he told Bobby. "These contracts violate laws and ethics."

"Frank," I cut in, "what can be done about it?"

"The first thing is to stop paying Albert any money at all. I'll write a letter challenging the validity of any contracts between them."

Bobby was stunned. The thought of challenging Grossman—of cutting him off—was beyond his imagination (and Bobby had a pretty vivid imagination). He looked at me like a small boy in trouble.

"What should I do, Louie?" he asked.

"Hire Frank and follow his directions," I said. "You finally have someone to protect your rights."

He returned to his old mantra: "Albert is the Bear. No one has ever beaten him."

"To quote somebody I know," I said, grinning, "'the times, they are a-changin'.'"

He smiled back. Then he hired Frank, and the war began.

The case went on for six years, and just before it was to go to trial, Grossman died of a heart attack on a flight to London. His wife, Sally, was his heir. Bobby contacted her and they reached a settlement in the case. Bobby got all his rights back. The Bear's tyrannical reign was over, and Mr. Tambourine Man had gotten justice.

I'm just glad I was there to intervene on my friend's behalf. Just as Walter Yetnikoff had not intimidated me, I knew that Albert Grossman was no "bear." I knew he wasn't beyond the facts or above the law, and that it was high time for Bobby to get back what was rightfully his. Albert was just another greedy, manipulative user hired to look out for the welfare of his client, but taking advantage of him instead.

Bobby didn't hide his gratitude for what Frank and I did. Unfortunately, though, Grossman did get one last laugh from beyond the grave. The silkscreen that Andy Warhol had given to Bobby, which he had traded to Grossman for an old sofa, ultimately found a new home. In 1988, Sally Grossman sold *Double Elvis* at auction for $720,000. In 2012, it sold again at auction—for $37 million.

TWENTY

Los Angeles Times

When I would go to Los Angeles in the late seventies, to get away from the Duluth winters and hang out with Bobby and other friends, I would stay at the Beverly Wilshire hotel. Sometimes I would have them over and we would party. On one of those occasions, everything was going along happily and a good time was being had by all. Among my many guests were my sister, Sharon; Kinky Friedman; and his girlfriend from Vancouver, Kacey Cohen. Kacey went into the bathroom and when she tried to come back out, she couldn't open the door. After repeated attempts, she got panicky and started to pound on the door, scream, and cry. We gathered outside, trying to help and yelling encouragement to her, but the door was locked from inside and just would not open.

I knew Kacey was feeling claustrophobic but I didn't want to call the hotel people because the place reeked of pot, and, in those days, this was a bigger deal than it is now. So I did what any good host would do. On a dark, foggy L.A. night, I climbed out the window onto an insanely narrow ledge. Then I inched my way toward the bathroom window and Kacey. When I looked down five stories to the street below, I said a little prayer asking God to protect His favorite fool, and kept going.

"Louie, what the hell are you doing?!" I heard my sister scream from behind me. "Get back in here! That's Kinky's girlfriend! Let Kinky rescue her!"

From the other window, I heard Kacey screaming. I was on a thin ledge high above Wilshire Boulevard with hysterical ladies screaming at me from both sides. As I contemplated which way to go, I could hear my mother's voice in my head saying, *Louis, always do the thing that will make your father and me proud.*

Rescuing a damsel in distress should qualify, I thought, as I forged ahead toward Kacey.

I managed to climb in the bathroom window, comfort Kacey, and jimmy open the door, to the cheers of the assembled multitudes.

"Louie, that was either the most courageous or the stupidest thing you've ever done in your life," Kinky said, genuinely in awe.

By the late seventies, I was spending more and more time in L.A., which had proved itself an ideal town for a bachelor. Most of my friends in Duluth were settled down with families, so up there, my social life consisted mainly of group dinners, with a few weekend fishing or ski trips thrown in. In L.A., I spent my nights going out to clubs like the Troubadour and Dan Tana's, or popping in on a house party. We'd end our long nights at Canter's Deli, where we'd sit around a big table talking and laughing until the wee hours of the morning. Duluth was my home, but L.A. was my playground, exciting in ways Duluth could never be.

One night, driving around on the West Side with Bobby, I told him that I knew this girl who was a Bunny at the Playboy Club in Century City. I wanted to stop by and say hello to her.

"Let's do it," he said.

When we got inside and found a table, I asked about the girl I knew (appropriately nicknamed "Bunny"), and soon she came hopping over to visit with us. The club offered live entertainment, and that night Lainie Kazan came on and gave a great performance. Bobby really liked the show and wanted to meet Lainie, so I asked Bunny to pass the word to the Playboy people that Bob Dylan was there. Would Lainie like to come by and say hello?

Of course, she came right over, and Bob and she got along great. Clearly, the admiration was mutual. Lainie's straightforward, New York-style outspokenness seemed somehow refreshing in California, and a long-term friendship was forged that night.

I'll say this about the Playboy Club. It's one of the few places I've ever gone with Bobby where he wasn't writing notes for a song.

If not for Bobby, I would never have had so many good times in L.A. I certainly wouldn't have won Tom Waits's lucky tie in a game of craps.

One night, as Dan Tana's was closing, a group of us were leaving at the same time as Tom Waits and his party.

As we milled around on the sidewalk of Santa Monica Boulevard, Tom and I started chatting.

Then he pulled out a pair of dice and said, "Do you want to play craps?"

"Sure," I said, and we both got down on our knees on the sidewalk. We each pulled out a wad of cash and started throwing the dice as our respective groups of friends gathered behind us to cheer us on. My dice were hot, and it wasn't too long before I'd cleaned Tom out of all the cash he had on him.

"Tom, if you don't have any more cash, I guess the game is over," I said.

"You can't leave!" he screamed. "You have all my money!"

"Well, I'm willing to keep playing, but you have to feed the pot."

"But ... I don't have anything to put in."

I looked him up and down and said, "How about that tie? Put that down, and we can keep playing."

"This is my trademark lucky tie! I can't do that!"

I shrugged and turned to leave, my pockets bulging with his cash.

"Don't leave!" he shouted as he removed his beloved tie and placed it gently on the sidewalk. "I swear to God, I am going to win back all my money and then some!"

With a smile, I picked up the dice.

"Baby needs a new pair of shoes, but will settle for Tom's tie," I said as the dice clicked onto the pavement and stopped at seven.

Another winning throw for me.

I picked up the tie and asked Tom if there was anything else he'd like to wager.

He shook his head and pulled his pants pockets inside out to show that they were empty.

"You can't leave with all my money *and* my tie," he whined.

"I can and I will," I said. "If you want to keep playing, put your hat in the pot."

"No! I can't lose my hat, too. I can't!"

"OK, then, Tom. Thanks for everything," I said as I walked away.

I could hear him screaming in anguish as I left with my friends.

Some years later, I was at the Hollywood Bowl for one of Bobby's concerts. When the show was over and the lights came up, I noticed Tom sitting about five rows in front of me. We locked eyes and both of us smiled. I wandered over to say hello, wondering if he still bore a grudge about that crap game.

As we shook hands, Tom said to his wife, "This is Louie Kemp. He has my tie!"

Of course, my business would never allow me to get totally swallowed up by L.A. During summers in the late seventies, I would travel to Western Alaska to take care of my seafood operation up there. One year, I met an incredible native artisan who made totem poles. They were about seven feet tall, magnificently colorful, with carved faces unique to each one. These were genuine works of art—so naturally, I bought one.

My original plan was to install the thing on my mother's front lawn in Duluth, but she expressed serious concern about what the neighbors would think. I ended up loaning it to the Tweed Museum of Art at UMD, to their great delight.

Once Bobby had finished his Malibu compound, I took it back from the University and had it shipped to California, where Bobby happily set it up facing the Pacific Ocean. My other housewarming gift to him was a functional antique Coke vending machine, which he installed in the foyer of his house. They were good presents for the friend who has everything (but not a totem pole)! I don't know if he nicknamed it "Quinn."

In 1978, Bobby did his first tour in Japan and invited me to join him. I did a lot of business over there, so I figured it would be a good opportunity to see some customers while traveling with Bobby.

A wild scene greeted us at the Tokyo airport. The press was there en masse, and they descended like locusts on Bobby. Gary, the security guys, and I had to surround him for protection. His press conference later that day was classic Dylan: cryptic, funny, and obtuse. The Japanese press hung on every word.

Bobby's first concert of the tour was at the Nippon Budokan arena, and afterward, Sony threw a party in his honor at a beautiful restaurant called Maxim's de Paris.

The buffet tables were brimming with bowls of caviar and ornately styled sushi. The guest list was drawn from the upper echelons of the Japanese business and entertainment worlds, and everybody was dressed to the nines. Bobby and I were, of course, in our blue jeans and leather jackets. At one point in the evening, a very distinguished-looking Japanese man came over, his suit impeccable and his English quite good. He shook Bobby's hand and said it was an honor to meet him, and an honor for the people of Japan that he had come to perform there. Flattered, Bobby thanked him, and asked his name.

The man smiled, straightened his posture, and puffed out his chest a little.

"I am Akio Morita, founder of the Sony Corporation."

Bobby thanked him again and congratulated him on his success. Mr. Morita smiled and offered a half bow of respect in return, then quickly took his leave. Bobby and I just looked at each other and exchanged the lift of an eyebrow.

We were staying at the Hotel New Otani in downtown Tokyo, a very imposing structure. From our rooms on a high floor, we could see the whole city spread out before us. We had made plans to go out to dinner on our second night with Bobby's then-manager, Jerry Weintraub. Jerry was a well-established L.A. entertainment mogul who'd produced record-breaking concerts for Elvis, John Denver, Frank Sinatra, and Neil Diamond, in addition to having managed Kinky for about fifteen minutes. He was also a successful movie producer, with *The Karate Kid, Diner,* and *Ocean's Eleven* to his credit.

We told Jerry to meet us at eight in Gary's room, which was next to Bobby's. We got there a little early, and were enjoying the view from Gary's window as we waited for Bobby to come over. We were relaxing and schmoozing, when—suddenly—a major earthquake hit.

The building swayed.

So did our stomachs.

I clutched the windowsill, figuring the whole structure was going to topple at any moment. Gary and I must have read the same articles about what to do in an earthquake, because we both ran over and stood under the arched doorway to the room. Jerry freaked out and ran down the hallway screaming. After what seemed like an eternity (but, in reality, was probably thirty seconds), it was over, and we were still alive.

Jerry came back into the room, having regained his composure.

"I've worked hard all my life, been very successful," he said. "It would be just my luck to die in an earthquake in Tokyo with Bobby. I can just see the *Los Angeles Times* headline: 'Bob Dylan and Entourage Die in Tokyo Earthquake.'"

Ten minutes later, Bobby came over, looking quite unruffled by the experience.

As we waited for the elevator, I said, "Bobby, what did you think of the earthquake?"

"What earthquake?" he said. He'd been playing the piano and was deep in Bob World. He hadn't even noticed it.

Jerry passed away in 2015, and when I saw his obituary

on the front page of the *Los Angeles Times*, I thought, *Man, you got your wish: your name in the headline, and no mention of Bob Dylan.*

Before 1978 was history, Bobby would release his album *Street Legal.* He had a rehearsal studio in Santa Monica, and decided he would record it there.

As preparations for the session were being made, Bobby said to his assistant at the time, Ava Megna, "I like the acoustics in the men's room. I might record the album in there."

Shortly after that, Arthur Rosato, his technician at the studio, wandered into Ava's office looking distracted, and mentioned that Bob had said as much to him. Ava didn't think this was the best idea Bob had ever had, so she made a quick call to Don DeVito at Columbia Records in New York. He was producing the album.

"You'd better get out here," she said. "Bob has an interesting idea about where he wants to record."

Don was there the next day.

For better or for worse, the record was made in the studio, not the men's room.

The liner notes on *Street Legal* included the following credits:

Champion of All Causes — Larry Kegan
Secretary of Goodwill — Ava Megna
Second in Command — Arthur Rosato
Special Thanks for Helping Out: Gary Shafner and Lou Kemp

In the mid-eighties, I had a hundred-foot supply boat as part of my Alaskan operation. I'd named it the *Frieda K* after my mother. At one point, the boat was on charter to an oil company working off the coast of Nome—which is very near Russian waters—in the Bering Sea.

I was shocked to get a call that the *Frieda K* had been boarded and seized by the Russian Navy, and hauled off to Siberia on suspicion that it was part of a spying operation. This became a widely reported international incident.

When it was made public that I was the owner of the vessel, the Duluth newspaper called and asked if they could interview the "real" Frieda K, i.e., my mother. I told them I'd ask her—and went on to say that the Russians were fortunate that they'd seized her namesake and not the original Frieda, as she would have kicked their asses.

"They'd have called me up and begged me to come get her," I said—and I was really only half kidding.

Frieda was one tough lady, while remaining one of the kindest, most generous people who ever lived. There's no question the Russians would have been outmatched by Frieda—but she never forgot to put a sweater on my German Shepherd Sam, so he wouldn't catch a chill in the Duluth winters.

TWENTY-ONE

Knockin' on Heaven's Door

Dan Tana's lounge on Santa Monica Boulevard was a favorite hangout for industry people. One night when I came in, I saw some of my friends sitting in a booth: David Blue, Season Hubley, and Harry Dean Stanton, among a few others, along with an African-American woman I didn't recognize. Harry introduced her as Mary Alice, and mentioned that she'd been in *Pat Garrett and Billy the Kid* with Bobby and him. She had a big personality and a great smile.

Gradually, it dawned on me that Bobby had mentioned her before, as a good actress and nice person. I walked over to the pay phone near the entrance and called Bobby at his house in Malibu. I told him that Mary Alice was at Tana's, and asked if he wanted to talk to her. When he said yes, I put the handset on top of the phone, walked back over to our booth, and caught Mary Alice's eye. Then I motioned to her to come with me. We hadn't really talked yet, so she pointed to herself as if to say, *Do you mean me?* I nodded, and she squeezed her way out of the booth.

"Someone would like to speak with you," I said. "Follow me."

Being a good sport, she shrugged and followed me to the phone, and I handed her the receiver without a word. She seemed pretty surprised by who was on the other end of the call. I hung back while she and Bobby chatted, and when she handed the phone back to me and returned to the booth, I asked Bobby if he wanted me to bring her out to see him in Malibu. He said yes, and suggested the following day.

Mary Alice was happy to accept Bobby's invitation, so I picked her up and took her out to Malibu as planned. It was the first of many visits, and sometimes I would join them. We would often end up at Canter's Deli or some other soulful place at two o'clock in the morning. Mary Alice was very spiritual, and was attending Bible classes at a place called the Vineyard School of Discipleship. At some point, she asked Bobby if he'd like to join her, and, being the curious type, he agreed to check it out.

The classes were all about the New Testament, and Bobby found the information enlightening and compelling. He ended up attending the full course with Mary Alice, which lasted about three months, and then he continued to study. He'd always felt a strong connection to spirituality, and the Bible study affected him deeply. Within the context of his own Judaism, he developed an appreciation and acceptance of Jesus.

It was 1980, and I was renting a condo on Wilshire Boulevard in Westwood. Many a night, I'd wake up to the sound of somebody pounding on the door. Bobby. I'd let him in and we'd sit at the kitchen table, talking endlessly about religion and life. Sometimes my girlfriend, Kimberly, would get up and bring us food to fuel the conversation.

At the time, Bobby was renting a house in Brentwood so he wouldn't have to drive an hour each way to Malibu every time he came into the city. He had plenty of room there, and suggested I give up my place and stay with him whenever I was in town. I ended up doing exactly that, and spending lots of time there—just talking, hanging out, and dreaming. (Those days would end when I got married, in February of 1983.) The conversations that had started at my kitchen table in Westwood moved over to Bobby's kitchen, where we continued to discuss spiritual matters. If you'd been a fly on the wall, you might've thought you'd stumbled into a seminar on comparative religion.

In December of 1980, I went back to Duluth to visit my mother. Knowing that I'd have a short layover at the Minneapolis airport, I asked my old friend Larry Kegan if he was free, and he said he would come out to see me.

When I got off the plane, sure enough, there was Larry in his wheelchair. On one side of him was his full-time assistant Alfonso ("the Holy Fonz"); on the other side was the imposing figure of an Orthodox rabbi in traditional dress, sporting a long beard.

Larry knew that I had a lot of spiritual questions about life, and I'd once asked him to keep his eyes open for a person who might be qualified to help me answer them. He'd met this rabbi and been impressed by his wisdom and righteous lifestyle—so when he found out I'd be passing through Minneapolis, he invited the holy man to come along to the airport. Being the selfless, giving person he was, the man agreed to come out in the minus-twenty-degree weather after having taught all day, to talk to a stranger about God. (His wife and fourteen children would have to wait.)

We found a table away from the bustle of travelers, and had a soul-searching talk. I had good questions, and Rabbi Friedman responded with great answers that awakened my mind and soul. As my flight to Duluth was being called, I thanked the man and made arrangements to sit in on his classes while I was in Minnesota.

After visiting with my mother for a few days, I drove down to the Twin Cities. Larry and Alfonso picked me up at my hotel and took me to Chabad House in Saint Paul, where Fonz and I carried Larry in his wheelchair up the stairs to the second floor. We quietly found seats at the back of the crowded classroom. The rabbi was already speaking, and the attentive students scribbled in their notebooks.

After about ten minutes, I whispered to Larry, "The class is all females!"

"Yes," he whispered back, "He only teaches women. You're the first guy he's ever invited to his class."

Hmm … quite a fringe benefit, I thought. And instead of staying a couple of days, as I'd planned, I attended class for three weeks. Rabbi Friedman was very nice about it, and even offered to meet with me privately after each session to answer any questions I might have.

As a result of my devotion to the course, I met Corinne— an exotic-looking French-Moroccan girl with big eyes, who was fluent in adorably accented English, French, and Arabic. She was from Casablanca, where Bogie had run Rick's Café in the movie that put the place on everybody's radar for all time.

On our first date, I took Corinne to see Johnny Cash at the Carlton House.

The next day, in class, she told her friends, "Louie took me to the Cash House to see Johnny Carlton."

Close enough. I married her two years later.

At my last meeting with Rabbi Friedman, he said, "If you look into the mirror, Louie, you might look the same. But you are no longer the same person you were when you walked through my door."

He was right.

"So ... what are you going to do about it?" he asked.

"I don't know, Rabbi."

"There are 613 commandments—"

"You can stop there," I said. "You have to understand, Rabbi, I grew up in Duluth, which has just a small Jewish population and no formal Jewish education. The only reason I know about the Ten Commandments is because of the movie—and I can't even keep all of *them*."

The holy man sat quietly for a moment, stroking his beard, then said, "There are five commandments which—if you keep them—will bring you into a much closer relationship with God. When I first met you at the airport, you said that you knew you were running up a big tab with God for all the good fortune He has given to you. You wanted to know how you could start paying Him back. If you adhere to these five commandments, you will be taking a big step toward paying off that tab."

The five things he told me I must do were, keep the Sabbath, keep kosher, put on tefillin and say my prayers each day, wear tzitzis (literally the "fringes" of the mini prayer shawl worn under men's clothes), and perform acts of tzedakah (charity).

He then explained to me the meaning of each of these commandments, physically, spiritually, and mystically. When he finished, we sat quietly as I pondered my spiritual path. The businessman in me thought I'd made a pretty good deal, having negotiated the rabbi down from 613 to five.

"Rabbi, I will follow these commandments," I said. "Starting now."

Back in L.A., living in the Brentwood house, I found the dynamics had become pretty interesting. I was now a practicing, observant Jew, while Bob was deeply involved in studying the New Testament. He had come to believe that Jesus truly was the son of God, who had come to Earth to receive our sins and die for them. He understood Jesus as part of the Holy Trinity: Father, Son, and Holy Ghost. I saw Jesus as a rabbi, teacher, and another Jewish boy who'd made good.

Nearly every day, Bobby and I would engage in intense discussions of theology. I soon realized I didn't have a deep enough knowledge of my faith to counter Bobby's arguments; I was outmatched. After one such discussion, I went to my room and called Rabbi Friedman. I told him I had a close Jewish friend who was absorbed in the New Testament, and that I didn't feel equipped to debate him. I asked if he would be willing to come to L.A. and meet with my friend, perhaps help him understand Jewish theology and traditions—the Jewish version of the meaning of life.

It had become my mission to help Bobby find the spiritual fulfillment his soul was yearning for in Judaism—the religion of his ancestors. (As it is written, God told Abraham, "I will bless and bring knowledge and light to the world through your seed.")

Rabbi Friedman agreed to help me in my quest to "bring Bobby home" spiritually, and to fly out to meet with him.

"Sure, bring him to the house," Bobby said when I told him about it, so I made arrangements to fly the rabbi to L.A. the following week.

Mind you, he had no idea who my friend was until he arrived. As it turned out, the two got along very well, and it was the beginning of Bobby's Jewish education. Once he dipped his toe in, Bobby developed an abiding passion for Judaism—while maintaining his profound appreciation for Jesus as a historical and spiritual figure. He stayed in touch with Rabbi Friedman and continued to meet with him over the years, in L.A., Minneapolis, and New York.

Speaking about his star pupil, the rabbi said, "In his innocence, the basic Jewish values that Bob had attained in his youth were rekindled when he started to study. It was all very natural for him to evolve a greater understanding and active observance of his Jewish faith."

I would introduce many more rabbis and observant Jews to Bobby, each bringing with him a brick to strengthen the foundation of his faith. Rabbi Bentov, a Kabbalist from Jerusalem who regularly stayed at my house in L.A., had a big spiritual impact on both Bobby and me. His wisdom and knowledge seemed almost supernatural, and are like sacred inscriptions on my heart. In retrospect, I wish I had taken all the advice and direction he gave me. When I ignored it, the consequences seemed to unfold just as he'd predicted.

I introduced Bobby to Rabbi Moshe Feller in Saint Paul, and he went on to study the Torah and Talmud with him. Rabbi Feller told Bobby and me some interesting stories. Apparently, he'd met Sandy Koufax the day after the Hall of Fame player had refused to pitch the first game of the 1965 World Series because it fell on Yom Kippur. Koufax invited Rabbi Feller up to his room at the Saint Paul Hotel. The rabbi and the star pitcher talked about the two subjects for which they shared a passion, baseball and religion, and the rabbi presented Koufax with a pair of tefillin—the sacred leather boxes containing scripture that Jewish men bind to their heads and arms during weekday prayers.

In the game that Koufax had sat out, his Los Angeles Dodgers were pitted against the Minnesota Twins. The great Don Drysdale was filling in for Koufax, but, as it turned out, he got pounded early. When manager Walter Alston walked out to the mound to pull him out, the right-hander reportedly said, "I know, Skip. You're wishing I was a Jew."

Aware that Koufax had to rest up so he could pitch the second game of the Series, the rabbi got ready to leave.

Koufax stopped him, and said, "You know, Rabbi Feller, they made a big fuss that I didn't pitch on Yom Kippur. I don't pitch on Rosh Hashanah either."

Bobby would sometimes come to High Holiday services with me at Chabad of Pacific Palisades. When he was on the road, he'd often go to services and Seders at a local Chabad. In New York, Larry, Bobby, and I would go to Crown Heights together to see the Lubavitcher Rebbe, the leader of Chabad, who held massive services for more than three thousand of the faithful. Although the services were in Yiddish and we didn't understand a word, the energy and charisma of the Rebbe seemed to penetrate our souls. We knew we were in the presence of a holy, righteous leader sent by God to enlighten the world.

Many people tell stories of how their lives were changed by the Rebbe's advice, and of the many miracles he performed. World leaders and people from all religions and walks of life would come to him for advice and counsel. On one occasion, Bobby and I were in attendance, flanking Larry in his wheelchair. The Rebbe picked Larry out of the crowd of thousands, smiled, and stared directly into his eyes with his own penetrating blue ones. He then raised his cup in Larry's direction and offered him a l'chayim—a toast to life. It was very unusual for the Rebbe to pick one person to honor publicly, and we all felt the weight of that moment.

Afterward, Bobby whispered to me, "I think the Rebbe likes Larry better than us."

"Yes," I agreed. "I guess when you can look into a person's soul, you don't care about their worldly accomplishments or possessions."

"Larry must outshine us spiritually," Bobby concluded.

We agreed we had to work on elevating our souls.

According to Rabbi Friedman, "Bobby fell in love with the Rebbe, having finally found someone he could look up to, somebody he could never compete with, who was not impressed with worldly acclaim."

When the Rebbe passed away, on June 12, 1994, Bobby gave an unsolicited, generous donation to Chabad of Minnesota in the great man's memory and honor.

Rabbi Feller told me another story:

"A few years ago, Bobby attended Yom Kippur services at our Chabad synagogue in Saint Paul. You can imagine the excitement his presence created. One young woman from out of town was a huge Dylan fan, but had given up the opportunity to visit Bobby's old home in Hibbing with her parents because it was Yom Kippur. She'd chosen instead to pray with us.

"When she rejoined her parents that evening, she let them go on and on about what she had missed up in Hibbing. When they finally calmed down, she said, 'You saw

Bob Dylan's house. I met Bob Dylan. He was at the synagogue that I attended!'"

Rabbi Feller continued reminiscing about his experiences with Bobby: "One way in which we prepare for Rosh
Hashanah," he said, "is by sounding the shofar after morning prayers. After Bob and I concluded one particular study
session, I invited him to accompany me onto our veranda,
where I sounded the shofar especially for him. It was a
particularly windy day, and when I'd finished sounding the
traditional calls of the ram's horn, I remarked, 'Bob, that's
the real 'Blowin' in the Wind.' He just smiled."

Over the years, the lessons Bobby learned in his spiritual
quest yielded some profound statements that have stuck
with me to this day.

"We are all spirits dressed up in a suit of skin," he once
said. "And we are going to leave all that behind. We have
to work out who we are down here, and where we fit in."

He and I were blessed to have studied with and been
guided by some amazing tzaddiks—holy men. We are different people because of it.

TWENTY-TWO

Family Man

It was 1983 and I was about to get married for the first time—to Corinne, whom I'd met when I audited Rabbi Friedman's all-female Torah class. The wedding was to be at my house in Duluth, and since it was February, there was a lot of snow on the ground. The temperature was minus twenty degrees with a wind chill of around minus thirty-five. In retrospect, I have to wonder why we didn't do it in July or August—but the weather didn't seem to deter our friends, who came from all over to attend: Seattle, Alaska, Japan, Los Angeles, Texas, Canada, Florida, and Chicago, as well as the Twin Cities.

Bobby, my best man, flew in from halfway around the world to be there, and stayed at my house. Rabbi Feller and Rabbi Friedman came up from Saint Paul to perform the Orthodox ceremony, during which Corinne and I stood under the traditional chuppah. In keeping with a custom that originated in the Kabbalah, she circled around me seven times during the ceremony. This is a ritual reenactment of the creation of the world, during which the earth made seven revolutions.

At the end of the ceremony, I stomped on and broke a glass wrapped in cloth, signifying the sorrow of the

Jews over the destruction of the original temple by the Romans some two thousand years ago. Before I did this, I said (in Hebrew), *If I forget thee, O Jerusalem, let my right hand be forgotten.* The right hand represents all the good things in life.

After I broke the glass, everyone shouted, "Mazel tov!" and the celebration began.

It felt wonderful to bring my loved ones together for this joyous occasion. The guests were a diverse lot. Mickey and Jeno Paulucci, my partners in an Alaskan seafood company, were there. So were Gary Shafner and his fiancée, Gay. Frank Berman, who was actively representing Bobby against ex-manager and shyster Albert Grossman at the time, was there as well. There were really too many people to mention by name, but I loved them all, and they all seemed to have a great time.

After the ceremony, which was held in front of a big bay window with a view of frozen Lake Superior, refreshments were served on the main floor. Then everyone descended to the lower level for a lavish kosher dinner. Food is a very important part of Jewish celebrations, and we had no intention of skimping on that tradition.

You won't be surprised to hear that among the offerings were smoked Lake Superior trout, Alaskan King salmon, and caviar, courtesy of my various companies. Barbecued chicken, brisket, lamb chops, and many types of salads and desserts rounded out the feast.

Once the crowd had thinned out and we were down to the inner circle, someone brought out an acoustic guitar. Kinky entertained everyone with a few of his songs,

Bill Graham, Marlon Brando, and I hanging out backstage at Bill's 1975 San Francisco benefit concert. I remained friends with both of them.

Bob is mobbed by paparazzi and fans as he gets off a plane in Japan to start his tour there. That's me to his left, helping the security guards protect him.

Bob standing with Rabbi
Friedman at my wedding.

Bob was the best man at my wedding in
1983. The ceremony and reception were at
my house in Duluth.

My best man walks
down the aisle.

Bobby coming up to congratulate Corinne and
me after the ceremony.

From left to right: Bobby, me, and my good friend Mickey Paulucci at my wedding.

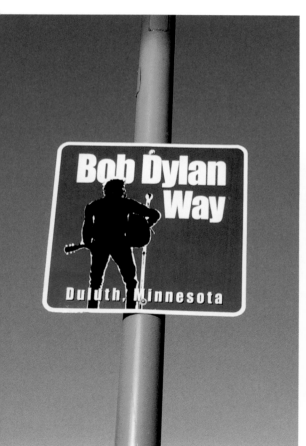

In 2006, Duluth, Minnesota dedicated a street to its most famous native son: Bob Dylan Way. *Photo by Phil Fitzpatrick*

The famous 110-year old Ariel lift bridge in the Duluth, Minnesota harbor. *Photo by Michael Anderson*

After Corinne and I decided we were better off as friends than as husband and wife, she introduced me to Anne, who would become my second wife.

My draft card. Most people rejected from the service receive a designation of "4-F." My card was stamped "E-6," and to this day, I don't know what it means. (I do remember the doctor at my preinduction physical shouting at me to "get the hell out and never come back!")

Left: One of the packages created for the company I founded and ultimately sold to Oscar Mayer.

Right: Bering Trader: My 350-foot seafood processing ship steaming out of the Seattle harbor, headed for Alaska.

My house in Duluth, bordered by Lake Superior to the south and Highway 61 to the north. It was here that I married Corinne.

My house in Pacific Palisades, where Anne and I got married. In the driveway sits the 1919 Rolls Royce I bought.

Left: Bob and Rabbi Bentov outside my Pacific Palisades house.
Right: Bob and Rabbi Cunin at the Chabad Telethon.

Larry and I were the only nonfamily members invited to Bob's fiftieth birthday party.

Spending time with Larry.

Bob with Rabbi Bentov.

Larry, Bobby, and me goofing around on the beach in Mexico.

Larry's tombstone. *Photo courtesy of Linda Passon-McNally*

including my favorite, "They Ain't Makin' Jews Like Jesus Anymore."

That number took us both back to a moment during "Rolling Thunder 2," when we were in New Orleans. We had a few days off and wanted to unwind a little, so Kinky and I and a few others went out to a club. The MC immediately recognized Kinky, and asked him to come on stage and sing a song. The crowd joined in, clapping and yelling for him to sing, but Kinky refused.

"It's my day off," he grumbled. "I'm not going up there."

I felt bad that he was going to disappoint the crowd, so I reached into my pocket and pulled out a hundred-dollar bill.

I waved it in front of his face and said, "Go up and sing 'They Ain't Makin' Jews Like Jesus Anymore' and this is yours."

Without a word, Kinky snatched that bill out of my hand and stomped up to the stage.

The crowd loved the song and so did I, and when the uproar died down, Kinky said, "It was a financial pleasure."

I would never have asked Bobby to play at my wedding, but he was enjoying himself immensely and, to the delight of the other guests, he grabbed a guitar that one of my Alaska management employees, Gerry Bee, had brought over and sang for quite a while. Larry was a pretty good singer in his own right, and offered up a few tunes as well. All in all, it was a pretty special night.

About a month after the wedding, an enormous package arrived from Bobby: a beautiful antique windup clock with chimes.

That April, he went into the studio and recorded the *Infidels* album, which includes "Jokerman" and "Neighborhood Bully," a powerful song about Israel. There is no doubt that our time spent studying with the rabbis had influenced him. Bobby was clearly returning to his Jewish roots, guided by his ancestors, the rabbis, the Rebbe, and the Torah itself.

Sixteen months after the wedding, Corinne and I received another gift—the best one of all. Our daughter Elana was born at St. Mary's Hospital in Duluth, the same hospital that had brought forth Bobby and me.

Bobby wasn't just my friend; he was often my soundtrack—especially in the car. When Elana was around seven, I would drive her to and from school in my black Jaguar, and Bobby's music was often coming out of the speakers. She became particularly mesmerized by "Tweeter and the Monkey Man," from the first album he recorded with the Traveling Wilburys (the supergroup he formed with George Harrison, Jeff Lynne, Roy Orbison, and Tom Petty). "What does it mean?" my little music-lover would ask me. She was particularly enthralled by the chorus.

I really didn't have an answer for her, but she continued to request the song every time we drove somewhere. Then one day, when Bobby was visiting us, she asked him about it.

"'Monkey Man' is my favorite song," she said, looking up at him with her big half-Moroccan-half-Polish eyes. "Will you please sing it for me?"

"What is it that you like about that song?" he asked her.

"I just like it," she said. "Even though I don't understand it."

Bobby wasn't in the habit of taking requests, but he'd known Elana since she was born—and has always been a fan of children and dogs—so he graciously sang her a few lines. He probably loved the fact that she accepted its mystery, just as all of his devoted fans always have.

I started a company in Duluth to make imitation king crab using a Japanese technique called *surimi*. I'd learned about it on one of my many trips to Japan, and figured there might be a market for it in the United States—and boy, was I right. The product became wildly popular in the States as a main ingredient in seafood salad, California rolls, and other dishes. I contracted with the Japanese manufacturer of the equipment to buy it from them, and they agreed to send their technicians to Duluth to train my people. I bought a 60,000-square-foot concrete building in West Duluth to house the operation. It had originally been Standard Oil Company's distribution center and offices, where Bobby's father, Abe Zimmerman, had worked when they lived in Duluth.

That office actually figures into the Dylan legend. As the story goes, Bobby gave his first public performance there at age three, standing atop his father's desk and singing into a Dictaphone. As I signed the papers for the building, I had no idea that I'd be manufacturing imitation king crab at the site where Bob Dylan made his first recording.

The crab operation was a big success, due in no small part to the fact that I'd followed the advice my father had given me about twenty years earlier, when he was training me in the fish business.

"Son," he'd said, "there are two ways to operate. Either you strive to produce the highest-quality product possible or you become a price seller. The second thing—trying to undercut your competitors on price—that won't work for the long term. Eventually there will be a faster gun, a prettier girl, and someone with a lower price. Quality is the only way to build and maintain a business long term."

With that in mind, I formulated my Crab Delights products using the highest-quality pollock and other ingredients, and the least amount of water possible. They were sold out of the refrigerated case so that they'd always be fresh and appealing. These high-quality products were well received by stores, consumers, and—unexpectedly—by the Oscar Mayer Company, the hot dog king. They had decided they wanted to get into the seafood business, but were only interested in the finest refrigerated products. Just as Abe Kemp promised, if you produce quality products, they will come.

At first I wasn't interested in selling, but the Oscar Mayer folks made me an offer so attractive I couldn't resist. Their headquarters was in Madison, Wisconsin—which was fine—and they seemed like very good and smart people. We were on the same page: quality is king. I sold the company to them and signed a five-year consulting agreement; they treated me very well.

In December 1987, one of my contacts at Oscar Mayer told me he had four fifty-yard-line seats for Super Bowl XXII, between the Broncos and the Redskins. Was I interested in having them?

Does a bear shit in the woods? I thought. Of course I was. I said I'd be quite happy to put them to good use.

I may not have mentioned it yet, but I'm a big football fan. My favorite team is the Minnesota Vikings, but even though they would not be playing, this was the Super Bowl—the big show. Bobby was a sports fan too, so my first call was to him. We had gone to Twins, Vikings, and North Stars hockey games together, and caught the Knicks at the Garden. When we went to see the North Stars play an exhibition game against the Russian national hockey team, Bob showed up wearing a gray Russian-military sheepskin hat with a five-pointed red badge emblazoned with a hammer and sickle. Maybe it was a nod to his Zimmerman grandparents, who were originally from Odessa. Mike Goldfine and Mickey Paulucci, two of my Duluth friends who sat with us, were quite amused, and were relieved when Bob cheered with us for the North Stars. In spite of our show of team spirit, Russia won 5–3.

"I've got four fifty-yard-line seats for the Super Bowl in San Diego," I said when Bobby picked up the phone. "Would you and one of your kids like to go with me?"

"Count us in," he said quickly.

I took my twenty-three-year-old son, Aaron, and Bob brought his son Jakob, nineteen. On game day, Bobby and Jakob came to my house in the Palisades. I'd arranged a ride for us to LAX, and a flight to San Diego. Any pro game is fun to go to, but the Super Bowl is the ultimate hyped-up happening. As we walked through the parking lot into the stadium and headed for our killer seats, people saw right through Bob's sunglasses and hoodie and said things like, "Hi, Bob," and "Great to see you; enjoy the game!"

The people sitting around us stared a little, but everyone was respectful and kept their distance, maybe because they could see he was with family and friends. Throughout the game, Bobby paid a lot of attention to Jakob. He was teaching him how to write songs at the time, and actually gave the kid some songwriting lessons during the game! The tips must have paid off, because years later, Jakob's own band, the Wallflowers, achieved great success in its own right. The band's album *Bringing Down the Horse*, reached number twelve on the charts and was followed by five other records, including two solo albums.

It was nice watching Bobby and Jakob bonding over music and football that day—and it turned out to be a great father-son day for all of us. In the end, Washington beat Denver 42–10.

After about four-and-a-half years, Corinne and I decided we were better suited to being friends than spouses, and we got divorced. About a year later, she called me and said she had met a really nice girl she thought I would like, named Anne. Corinne knew me pretty well, so I figured, why not?

Anne turned out to be a beautiful five-foot-ten blonde, who was smart, spiritual, and lovely in every way. She was about to get her Ph.D. in psychology. We were engaged seven months later. When I told Bobby I was planning to take the plunge into marriage again, he got all concerned about me. One evening, he dropped by the house to give me the third degree: Was I sure I was doing the right thing? How long had I known her? What did I know about her and her family? His concern was consistent with the loyalty and friendship we'd always shown each other.

We were sitting on a leather couch in the breakfast nook discussing all this when Anne walked in.

She hadn't yet met Bobby so I introduced them and, without missing a beat, he asked her, "So why do you want to marry Louie?"

"Because I love him," she replied.

"Well, there certainly is a lot to love," said Bobby. "This mansion, another mansion in Duluth, fancy cars, lots of money and goodies. It must be easy to love Louie."

I could see that she was taken aback.

Her voice trembling and a bit indignant, she said, "I love Louie for *who he is,* not for *what he has!* I don't need his money. My family has more money than he has."

Then she ran out of the room crying.

Bobby and I sat in silence for a few minutes. Then he gave me that raised eyebrow and half-assed grin of his.

"You know," he said, "I think she really does love you. I think it's going to be good."

Two months later, we got married at my house. Anne and I both really liked Bobby's ballad from *Planet Waves* called "Wedding Song," so I planned a little surprise. When we were under the chuppah, the song came on over the speaker system. The rabbi paused the ceremony for the five minutes it took to play it from beginning to end, and then it was back to the business of becoming husband and wife.

Over the next few years, work and family kept me very busy. Anne and I had four kids, and Bobby is godfather to two of them, Sarah and Avi. What Bobby had said to me about parenthood that long-ago day on the beach in the Hamptons came back to me often as the kids grew: being a father really is the greatest thing.

My friend Amy from Minneapolis was staying with us for a few days while she was in L.A. on business. Amy was an accomplished young woman as well as a stunning model. One afternoon while she was there, Bobby dropped by and the three of us were talking. Somehow, my mother's name came up, and Bob said how much he liked and respected her. It reminded me of a story I just had to share with them.

When I graduated high school in 1960, the Vietnam War was raging and everyone had to register for the draft. I did so, of course, but luckily, I was able to get a four-year student deferment.

Down at school in Miami, about six weeks before the end of my final quarter, I got a call from my mother. She

said I'd gotten a notice from the draft board that my deferment was up, and I would have to go for my preinduction
physical in a couple of weeks at a local Miami facility. A
week later, she called again and said she was sending me
some information to take to my physical. It would be arriv-
ing special delivery, and would include a sealed envelope
from Dr. Harrington, our longtime family doctor.

"What's in the envelope, Ma?" I asked, curious about
what she was up to.

"Don't worry about it," she said. "And don't open it. Just
give it to the doctor at your physical."

I started to argue with her about it, saying it didn't feel
right to be handing the guy a "doctor's note" of some kind,
but she started to cry. I never could stand to hear her cry.

"OK, OK," I said. "Calm down. I'll do it."

She made me promise I wouldn't open the envelope.

A week later, I reported to the Miami National Guard
Armory, as directed, and found about a thousand other
guys ahead of me. The examinations were being han-
dled in assembly-line fashion: "Slam, bam, you're drafted,
man."

When my turn finally came and I went into the little
cubicle to see the doctor, I waved the envelope in front of
me and said, "Excuse me ... before we go any further, this
is from my doctor."

He grabbed the letter out of my hand, ripped open the
envelope, and started to read.

After maybe twenty seconds, he screamed at me,
"WHO THE HELL DO YOU THINK YOU ARE?!

The U.S. Army doesn't make special accommodations for anyone! If you think we're going to give you a silk uniform, you're crazy!"

I just gaped at him in shock.

He turned around, reached for a stamp on the shelf behind him, and smashed it down onto my draft card—*kaTHUNK*.

Then he threw it in my direction, along with the letter—which he'd crumpled into a ball—and said, "Get the hell out of here and never come back!"

His rant had captured the attention of everybody within earshot, and when I exited the cubicle, they stared in my direction.

What the hell had Dr. Harrington written?

I smoothed out the letter and read the following lines:

To Whom It May Concern:
Louis is allergic to wool. He is more than happy to serve,
but unless he is given a silk uniform, he will have an
allergic reaction. He must be given a silk uniform.

God's honest truth, I am allergic to wool. But only a mother—only *my* mother—would figure out how to use that fact to get me out of serving in the Army.

I got into my metallic-silver-blue Oldsmobile Starfire convertible and drove back to Coconut Grove in a state of shock.

When I called my mother, before I could say anything, she said, "They don't want you, right? Always listen to your mother."

Knowing Frieda, Bobby and Amy cracked up at the story.

Then Amy turned to Bobby and asked, "Bob, did you get drafted?"

"I got rejected," he said. "Flat feet."

TWENTY-THREE

Homeless on Yom Kippur

Because of my deep connection to Chabad, I decided to make my house in Pacific Palisades into a Chabad House. We had Shabbat services, Passover Seders, classes, bar mitzvahs, weddings, and singles parties there for as many as five hundred people. About a week after one of those parties, a man came to my door and said he was a representative of some of my neighbors. They wanted to make an offer on my house: the sum he mentioned was a million more than I'd paid for it just a year before.

"Why?" I asked, taken aback.

"I'll be honest with you, Mr. Kemp," he said. "Before you moved in, this was a quiet neighborhood. Now, it seems like every other day you're hosting these big events ... people coming in and out ... God knows who they are. We're just not happy about having a lot of strangers here. In fact, it scares us."

I had to laugh.

"Listen, my friend," I said. "Please go back and tell my neighbors that they have no reason to be afraid. That is, unless the thought of a bunch of Jewish doctors, lawyers, accountants, students, and rabbis getting together for religious observance keeps them awake at night. Thank them for the generous offer, but tell them it's a *no* from their neighbor Louie."

At one point, Rabbi Cunin, head of Chabad on the West Coast, asked me if I could arrange for Bobby to perform at the annual Chabad Telethon, held to help fund Chabad's extensive charitable activities for people of all backgrounds. When I told Bobby about Cunin's devotion to the Rebbe and good relationship with Rabbis Friedman and Feller, he agreed to participate, and did so for several years.

In 1986, Bobby was in England at the time of the Telethon, so he sent a video of himself instead. In 1989, we formed an impromptu "supergroup" for the event: Bobby, his son-in-law; Peter Himmelman; and Harry Dean Stanton performed "Hava Nagila," after a quick practice at my house. Bobby played harmonica while Peter and Harry Dean sang.

In 1991, Bobby—wearing a yarmulke under his cowboy hat—accompanied Kinky on guitar while he sang "Sold American." Kinky told me later that Bobby had suggested they do another one of his songs, "Proud to Be an Asshole from El Paso," but Kinky didn't think it would fly with that crowd.

"Not doing 'Asshole' with Bob Dylan," Kinky confided later, "is the only major regret of my life."

In the nineties, when I was having some financial troubles, Bobby asked, "Don't you wish you still had all of those millions you donated to charity?"

I looked him in the eye and replied, "My only regret is that I didn't give more. I believe you can't take it with you, but you can send it ahead."

Bobby looked puzzled so I explained.

"Bob, what I gave to charity is in my family's account in Heaven. It will benefit us for eternity."

I really believe that.

A generous guy in his own right, Bobby shook his head in disbelief, surprised that I took such a long-term view and had such rock-solid faith in something I could neither see nor touch. Now, don't get me wrong; Bobby has always been very spiritual and generous, for instance, his donation in memory of the Lubavitcher Rebbe, which I mentioned earlier. He has also been known to do things for his own spiritual nourishment. Here's an example:

It was Yom Kippur, the Jewish Day of Atonement, at the tail end of the 1980s. Bobby was attending services at Chabad House in Santa Monica. Presiding was the venerable Rabbi Avraham Levitansky, beloved and revered by his congregation.

We had been there before, and the rabbi recognized Bobby right away, but few if any of his fellow worshippers—all somberly dressed—realized he was standing at the back of the room. Having, as usual, missed the memo regarding the dress code, Bobby was wearing cowboy boots, torn jeans, a hoodie, a black leather jacket, and what looked like a long-lost pair of Jackie Kennedy's sunglasses.

Specifically, he was attending the Neilah service. In Hebrew, *Neilah* means "closing the gate." As the day of Yom Kippur comes to a close and our future is being sealed, we turn to God to offer our repentance and new resolutions, and ask that He seal us in the Book of Life. We ask Him to grant us a new year replete with goodness and happiness.

The Neilah ends with the blowing of the shofar and the prayer that includes, "Next year may we be in Jerusalem."

The Ark housing the holy scrolls of the Torah remains open for the entire service, and it is considered a great honor to be chosen by the rabbi to open it. This carries with it many blessings for the new year. The honor customarily goes to the temple's most generous donor—but not this time. With his ancient eyes, Rabbi Levitansky scoured the congregation. At last, his gaze came to rest upon a solitary figure standing in the back of the room. He motioned the casually dressed fellow up to the pulpit, and up he came.

Bob Dylan opened the Ark on Yom Kippur.

Afterward, when the last echo of the shofar had diminished to silence and most of the congregants had trickled away, the biggest donor to the temple sought out Rabbi Levitansky and pulled him aside.

"I want you to know, Rabbi," said the man, "that when you didn't call me up to open the Ark, I was quite hurt. Then I saw whom you chose and I realized you were even wiser and kinder than I'd imagined. So I'm going to double my contribution for the coming year. It takes a great and generous heart to give the honor of opening the Ark for Neilah to a homeless Jew."

The rabbi has long since passed away, taking his spiritual secrets with him. As for the donor, unless he reads it here, he still doesn't know that the "homeless Jew" was Bob Dylan.

TWENTY-FOUR

Shalom, Amigo

Larry, who loved to get his friend's records on the day they were released, was in his van heading to a record store in Minneapolis to buy Bobby's *Love and Theft*. The date was September 11, 2001. More than a thousand miles away, the Twin Towers were falling after a heinous act of terrorism. Just like the thousands of innocent people who lost their lives that day, Larry Kegan was full of life one moment, and senselessly, abruptly dead the next—the victim of a fatal heart attack en route to the record store. I can safely say that Larry—in spite of the handicap he'd been living with so gracefully for decades—created as large a hole in this world with his departure as any one of those others did. Certainly in my world, and in Bobby's.

I got the bad news shortly after it happened, and called Bobby immediately. Of course, I told him where Larry had been headed on his last ride. We lingered on the phone, reminiscing about our beloved friend and then talking about the attacks in New York and Washington, and the downed plane in Pennsylvania. I told Bobby where Larry was going to be buried, and he said he intended to visit privately and say his good-byes at some point after the funeral. It was a scary and uncertain time for everyone, and the temporary ban on flying complicated matters. We mourned our friend while watching the news in our separate spaces, in numb disbelief, waiting for answers.

In death as in life, I felt close to Larry. We shared the same birthday—same day and year, both in Minnesota. We had the same initials. We were both descended from the Kohanim, a sacred Jewish tribe of priests comprising fewer than five percent of all Jews.

In Jewish tradition, the dead must be buried quickly— even in the face of a national tragedy that makes travel impossible—so I wouldn't be able to attend the September 12th service in person. Instead, I composed a eulogy and emailed it to one of our Minnesota friends, requesting that it be read during the service.

As it was later described to me, at one point the rabbi suggested, "God called Larry to Heaven to help disabled victims make their transitions to Eternity. He couldn't have picked a better man for the job."

I loved the thought of that. On many occasions when I'd been out with Larry, I'd toasted him by saying, "Larry, you'll be flying around in Heaven and walking in this world, for sure."

"Do you really think so?" he'd say.

"I guarantee it," I'd answer. "I can't tell you which will occur first, but they will both happen."

Our sages teach us that when the Messiah comes, there will be a resurrection of the righteous. It is clear to me that

Larry will be walking and strutting his stuff among them. I only hope I'll be there to witness it.

A few years after Larry passed, the rabbi of his congregation—Rabbi Zeilingold—and I arranged for a headstone to be erected, and I wrote the epitaph to be carved on it:

The best of the best
Always had a smile, a song
Good advice and love for all
Larry is now flying in Heaven
And he will be walking in this world
After the restoration of life

Shalom, amigo. Bobby and I love you eternally.

TWENTY-FIVE

Boys from the North Country

Writing this book has inspired me to search the long hallways of my memory and the depths of my soul. In the process, it has become clear to me that each experience and adventure Bobby and I shared has taken on a life of its own. As I write our stories down, they come alive again and become a sacred testament of life between friends. Truth and love cannot be denied or erased; they rise relentlessly to the surface and prevail, no matter what turns our lives take. The glue that has sustained our friendship is the fact that we have each been successful in our own endeavors while trusting and respecting each other unwaveringly. We have laughed at the same jokes, shared a love of God, and we have never forgotten where we came from. We both believe that we are all equals in God's eyes.

Our journey together started at summer camp. Our adventures have remained alive in both our hearts, and now they live on the page for all to share and remember. I think we both understand what a good thing that is.

In 2016, Bobby was awarded the Nobel Prize in Literature. He did not publicly respond or comment about it for over two weeks, which caused quite a stir among the Nobel Committee and others. Some thought he was being rude, disrespectful, arrogant—and it's easy to see how they might. You'd have to know Bobby to truly understand how he felt at that moment.

Bobby understood that his selection was far from conventional—as is his body of work. He isn't a "man of letters" in the usual sense. His gifts to the world, his work as well as his life, are unique. And the path that led him to that honor has taken many unconventional turns.

Having built a big following among folk-music enthusiasts, he chose the 1965 Newport Folk Festival to go electric—against the advice of many.

"Well, fuck them if they think they can keep electric out of here," he said at the time. "I'll do it."

Though it angered some followers who considered themselves "purists," Bobby's artistic bravery ultimately broadened his audience exponentially. He would go on to break every supposed "rule" in the music business. "You can't write songs that are longer than two or three minutes," he was told. "They won't get any airtime!" His "Like a Rolling Stone," which clocks in at around six minutes, went to number one on the charts. Other Dylan hits include "It's Alright, Ma (I'm Only Bleeding)" (seven-and-a-half minutes), "Hurricane" (eight-and-a-half), and "Desolation Row" (eleven-and-a-half).

Bobby has always done it his way. On May 12, 1963, he was set to perform on *The Ed Sullivan Show*, the most popular variety show of its time—maybe all time. It was on

Ed Sullivan that Elvis and the Beatles made their national TV debuts. *Ed Sullivan* was a career-maker.

During a rehearsal on the day of the show, Bobby was asked not to perform the satirical "Talkin' John Birch Paranoid Blues." The lyrics, he was told, were too controversial. Rather than change his set list, Bobby withdrew from the show altogether, unwilling to let Ed Sullivan and CBS dictate what song he could sing.

Bob's approach to his fans and followers and those who would praise him has never been conventional either. He sees himself as a conduit, a caretaker for a gift given him by God. He has never asked for approbation or honor from anyone or any group, in an industry that thrives on such things.

It is easy to get confused in this world, which is why I think clarity is such a special blessing. It is a blessing bestowed on Bobby, without a doubt. When it came time to accept the Nobel Prize, he asked a kindred spirit and fellow artist—the brilliant Patti Smith—to sing "A Hard Rain's A-Gonna Fall." After her beautiful rendition, the American ambassador to Sweden stepped forward to deliver the words Bobby had prepared. In his talk, Bobby paid tribute to all of his influences, literary as well as musical. He ended with the line, "I return once again to Homer, who says, 'Sing in me, oh Muse, and through me, tell the story.'" The words he composed for that day, as much as the lyrics to his songs and the stories in this book, form a map of who Bob Dylan is.

Some wonder why the Jews have been so successful in so many areas, including the arts. I believe that it is at least in part because the quest for knowledge, meaning, and truth are ingrained in our culture. We have a passion to seek out meaning and give it new expression, morally and artistically. That drive—along with another Jewish trait known as chutzpah—have always been strong in Bobby, and his gifts have made his expression worthy of the ages.

Bobby has been performing about one hundred concerts a year for the last thirty years, on something that has been referred to as "the never-ending tour." I once asked him why he tours so much.

"That's what I do," he said. "I don't know anything else. I'm not an electrician, carpenter, plumber, or a fish guy like you."

Bobby is more enlightened than most in those other professions—certainly more than the masterminds behind the RMS *Titanic* who arrogantly declared it "unsinkable." I bring that up because I'm thinking about an observation Kinky once made: "It was professionals who built the *Titanic*. It was amateurs who built the ark."

Recently, I was visiting with Joni Mitchell at her house in Los Angeles. I told her about writing this book, and we took our own stroll down memory lane. We were both astonished by the fact that our shared experiences have spanned nearly forty-five years. As Joni sipped her nightly "calm-your-ass-down tea," we laughed about an incident that happened during the "Rolling Thunder Revue" tour.

Joni had flown in with her manager, Elliot Roberts, to attend a few of our early concerts. Bobby invited her to come onstage and sing, and the crowds were thrilled by her great talent and incandescent charm. She was clearly having a great time, so I wasn't surprised when Elliot took me aside and asked if Joni could stay on the tour.

Naturally, we were thrilled to say yes, but Elliot had one concern. He had to be on the road with another client, Neil Young, and wouldn't be able to accompany Joni. I promised Elliot I'd look out for her myself.

Later in the tour, as we were crossing the border into Canada, everyone had to leave the buses and go into the Canadian customs building to clear customs. Standing in line, Joni realized she had some pot in her purse—a big no-no back then—and quickly discarded it. Wouldn't you know it? Someone on the Canadian side saw her do it and snitched to customs. Two men in uniform promptly took Joni into a room to interrogate her.

When I got wind of it, I went to the customs officials and advocated for Joni, pointing out that we had not yet entered Canada when she disposed of her little stash. After going back and forth with them a bit, they agreed to let her into Canada. Thank God. Because I'd had visions of having to call Elliot and tell him that the tour was going great—except for the part about Joni being in jail.

While my friendships with Joni and others sprang from Bobby, my friendship with Bobby and Larry came from somewhere else. As we grew from North Country boys into men, we shared a set of values and a simple outlook on life that transcended our individual success, values that had drawn us close and kept us close no matter the geographical distance. We saw one another from the inside out, not the outside in as others did. In spite of everything—and due in part to the fact that we had one another—we remained true to those young boys from northern Minnesota. We'd never felt the need to cut our fingers and mix our blood together to affirm our covenant. Our friendship was sealed with our shared values, actions, and adventures together.

My closeness to Bobby has never had all that much to do with music—any more than it has revolved around fish. I was never Bobby's fan, groupie, critic, commentator, or employee. He's always had plenty of those. Ours is a friendship based on mutual respect and appreciation. And love. We have always had open minds, taken risks, helped the underdog. We have laughed at the same jokes and confided our deepest thoughts and fears. We have never needed anything from each other, but have always been there for each other.

Neither of us has ever questioned the other's motives or agenda. Once Bobby had become Mega Bob and I had become very successful in my own way, others in our lives had agendas … that went with the territory. But we have always felt safe with each other in the way that only the closest of friends can. When one of us has needed a dose of truth, we've always known who to turn to.

Like most close friends, we had our disagreements. We worked through them, and ultimately, they made our friendship stronger. Either one of us would have taken a bullet—or a rotten tomato—for the other.

I have to end with a few words directed at the two best friends a man could be lucky enough to have.

Larry,

Please put in a good word for us upstairs, and stake out a cool spot for us all to hang out … preferably one with a view of planet Earth and the Milky Way. Also, please grab a few super-charged sets of wings so we can have races to the stars and back.

I am curious about the dating situation up there. When you get a chance, send me some details in a dream—and if you have a girlfriend, see if she has some nice friends for us.

I don't know if you've heard, but Bobby won the Nobel Prize in Literature. It's a pretty big thing, as you might recall. But you know Bobby, always an eager student, so if there is a long waiting list up there to enroll in a writing program, put Bobby on it. I am sure he would like to get some insights and answers in addition to those he's found "blowin' in the wind."

• • •

Bobby,

It is obvious that God loves you and has chosen you out of billions of people to bring special light and knowledge to this world. May He be pleased with how you have used this gift, and bless you in this world and the world to come with pleasure and peace.

Love,
Louie

DO IT YOUR WAY.

WE DID!

—

Louie

www.dylanandme.com
louie@dylanandme.com

The End